Center for Basque Studies
Current Research Series, No. 8

Violence and Communication

Edited by
Jose Antonio Mingolarra, Carmen Arocena, and Rosa Martín Sabaris

Current Research Series No. 8

Center for Basque Studies
University of Nevada, Reno

Published in conjunction with the University of the Basque Country
UPV/EHU

Current Research
Selections of the ongoing work done by the faculty of the University of
the Basque Country (UPV/EHU), www.ehu.es

Editorial Committee
Amaia Maseda (Chair, UPV/EHU), Arantza Azpiroz (UPV/EHU), Javier
Echeverría (Ikerbasque-UPV/EHU), Jon Landeta (UPV/EHU), Sandra Ott
(UNR), Joseba Zulaika (UNR), Santos Zunzunegui (UPV/EHU)

Current Research Series No. 8
Center for Basque Studies
University of Nevada, Reno
Reno, Nevada 89557
http://basque.unr.edu

Library of Congress Cataloging-in-Publication Data

Violence and communication / edited by Jose Antonio Mingolarra,
Carmen Arocena, and Rosa Martin Sabaris.
p. cm. -- (Current research series ; No. 8)
"Published in conjunction with the University of the Basque Country."
Includes bibliographical references and index.
ISBN 978-1-935709-22-0 (pbk. : alk. paper)
1. ETA (Organization) 2. Terrorism--Spain--País Vasco. 3. Violence--
Spain--País Vasco. I. Mingolarra, Jose Antonio. II. Arocena, Carmen. III.
Sabaris, Rosa Martin.

HV6433.S7V56 2012
363.3250946'6--dc23

2012012066

Contents

Introduction: Other Winds, New Dreams

Jose Antonio Mingolarra

Translated by Cameron J. Watson

There are times when a delay in the appearance of a work takes on a special, and in this case extremely encouraging, dimension. When this book was first conceived, any glimmer of hope that ETA violence might end was in its earliest days, and most people did not hold out any hope that this would happen. But the Basque Country's dreams of a nonviolent future, which we now trust to be definitive, have once more returned, and with them we welcome new way of constructing reality.

This book, which because of the change that has taken place in our immediate surroundings might appear to be of less significance, maintains all the vigor and importance it did when it was drawn up. This vigor and importance serve to understand—not forget, and not repeat our violent past—so that we can reconcile ourselves as a community paying special attention, care, and respect to the victims; so that any disregard of violent events beyond the reach of our own lives does not take root among us; and so that we might help the disappearance of such episodes by intervening from the place we know, which is that of the written word.

This book begins with "The Four Horsemen of the Apocalypse: Audiovisual Models of Representing Violence," by Imanol Zumalde. Here, Zumalde explores the phenomenon of violence from the perspective of its forms of expression and argues that the formidable visibility violence exhibits in our iconosphere is due in great part to an "effectiveness of symbols" question. In the pages that follow, and based on relevant examples, he describes the formal mechanisms that give rise to those patterns or aesthetic models in which audiovisual inscriptions of barbarism are found.

Once these bases for interpreting violent phenomena have been established, Zumalde also examines the expression of violence in its confrontation with "the different": in gender violence, in the relationship between poverty and violence, and so on. He concludes the chapter by looking at the way ETA violence is represented in Basque Country media, opening the door to regenerating a new social body through the resilience and forgiveness of victims.

In chapter 2, "The Construction of the Stranger and Social Violence," Imanol Zubero details extremely clearly how ethnic cleansing, the elimination of the different, is only possible among the ruins of a community of mutual acceptance. Genocides, the maximum expression of violence, are only possible after a long process of the social production of difference, a prior condition for the social production of moral indifference. Faced with the political construction of "the stranger," Zubero calls for the need to encourage processes of inclusion founded on the ethical and political relevance associated with neighborliness, the consciousness of coexisting in the same space.

Violence against women is another important area of study, and such expressions of violence, though not always evident and visible, can be nevertheless constant. In chapter 3, "In the Limbo of the Invisible," Carmen Arocena and Nekane E. Zubiaur attempt to visualize this seemingly invisible violence, demonstrating that violence against women is not always explicitly represented in the media. That dialectic between the visible and the invisible that the masculine outlook establishes in the media still impedes today, in the twenty-first century, access to a free and reliable expression of women's intellectual, physical, and sexual nature.

Coverage of violent conflicts has always been a theme of special attention because of its transcendence in shaping public opinion as well as the development of the conflicts themselves. In recent decades the changes experienced by these conflicts have made attempts to communicate them inadequate. The objective of chapter 4, "New Reference Points for Communicating Violent Conflicts: Poverty and Inequality and Positions in the Current Debate on the Causes of Civil Wars," by Alfonso Dubois, is to present the necessary references to understand current conflicts and to elaborate a communication that might help to better diffuse them. Specifically, Dubois emphasizes the need to understand the links between poverty and conflict as a key element. These conflicts have seen their media representations become events themselves. This is a question of understanding the need to comprehend the links between poverty and conflict as a key element, demonstrating the causal relations between civil war and poverty and inequality, and how international terrorism has modified strategies of national and international security.

Likewise, in this era of rapid Internet development, together with the difficulties involved in regulating online content, there is a lot of social unease with the notion of the Internet being "out of control" and outside the boundaries of legality, a place in which anything violent can easily take refuge. Such worries are multiplied when they refer to the most vulnerable groups, such as minors. Basing their findings on the European Union research initiative EU Kids Online, Maialen Garmendia, Carmelo Garitaonandia, Gemma Martínez, and Miguel Ángel Casado, the authors of chapter 5, "Violence and the Internet: New Technologies, Old Problems," analyze the media's role in shaping the Internet's image and its influence in how parents perceive the Web. Although to different degrees according to different countries, most media ignore the possibilities the Internet offers minors and center their discourse on existing threats, linking the Internet to violence, harassment, pornography, and so on.

How can one survive violent situations and learn to live freely again? Among the different forms of violence, terrorist violence is unusual in provoking proportionately more physical, social, psychological, and emotional shock—all characteristics that are difficult to overcome. Psychology seeks to identify elements that can repair victims' hurt. Resilience is at present a fashionable object of study, as it's a place in which people who have suffered some trauma can recover and even positively improve themselves through projects of stability, recovery, and transformation. In chapter 6, "The Psychosocial Recovery Processes in Victims of Violence and Terrorist Acts," Juan de Dios Uriarte demonstrates with his well-known precision how resilience is opposed to any trace of personal revenge. Achieving this requires a collective attitude based on social cohesion, cultural identity, governmental honesty, communicative management, and an important support for victims, so that once the damage is repaired, they are in a position to concede forgiveness.

While throughout the preceding chapters the violence this small country has suffered—I am referring to ETA violence—makes some kind of appearance, whether in a latent or more explicit way, the remaining chapters more clearly analyze the way in which the media has addressed politically violent events in the Basque Country.

In chapter 7, "Getting Closer: Photography, Death, and Terrorist Violence in the Basque Country," Ramón Esparza and Nekane Parejo relate an attack, the first of its kind according to some authors, which took place on June 27, 1960, and which resulted in the death of Begoña Urroz Ibarrola, a twenty-two-month-old baby girl. The secrecy imposed on this event by both ETA and General Franco's dictatorship made this act a dark place in the collective memory. The authors explain how regulating visibility is a basic characteristic of totalitarian regimes and how an appearance in the media (especially the audiovisual media) allows for the visibility of these kinds of events, as demonstrated in the chapter.

The title of chapter 8, "The Basque Press and Terrorism, 1990–2009: From Telling the Facts to Complicity against ETA," by José Ignacio Armentia and José María Caminos, clearly indicates its focus. Here, the authors demonstrate the steps taken by the Basque press from merely informing about mortal attacks by ETA to condemning these attacks. The chapter points out, by means of texts and graphs, how the *El Correo Español*, *Deia*, *Egin-Gara*, and *El País* newspapers conveyed mortal attacks by ETA in 1990, 2000, and 2009.

Chapter 9, "Humor, Violence, and Infotainment in the Basque Country: The *Vaya Semanita* Phenomenon on Basque Public Television, 2003–2005" by Carmelo Moreno, concludes the book. Moreno's argument is based on the fact that, historically, political information in the Basque Country has been polarized and governed by patrons of seriousness, marked undoubtedly by the terrorist experience, in such a way that in recent decades it has been very difficult to find any kind of humorous practice in public life. However, the situation is now different, and there are certain humorous programs on the radio and television broadcast in the Basque Country. One such show is *Vaya Semanita* (What a Week), which has enjoyed high audience ratings for Euskal Telebista (ETB, Basque public television) since it first appeared in 2003.

Moreno's hypothesis is that this show's success in the Basque Country reveals the triumph of a certain political discourse, in a relaxed and apparently moderate way. In order to test this hypothesis, he analyzes the content of the show's first two seasons (2003–2005) through discussion groups, to see the program's impact and how these groups interpret this. The end result demonstrates that, thanks to this comic attitude when it comes to "informing" about Basque politics, this infotainment show worked insofar as it helped to reinforce certain stereotypes about Basque politics, especially those shared by a majority of people. Likewise, these stereotypes served to place the more radical and serious political discourses in ridiculous and minority situations.

Conscious of the fact that examining the pairing of violence and communication is an arduous, complex, incomplete, and perhaps impossible task, this volume in the Current Research series seeks to visibly demonstrate certain generic and other particular aspects of the expression and representation of violence, especially terrorist violence in the Basque Country.

1

The Four Horsemen of the Apocalypse: Audiovisual Models of Representing Violence

Imanol Zumalde

Translated by Jennifer R. Ottman

Iconic Inflation and Symbolic Efficacy

Scholars from all social science branches point to the atavistic impulse toward violence as one of the great problems facing the world in which we live. This consensus is explained to a great extent by the omnipresence and interconnectedness of the phenomenon, which, without distinctions of any kind, is evident on the individual, group, and state levels. As political scientists and politicians of all stripes have been warning for some time, violence is also making its presence dramatically known in the macro-structural sphere of civilizations. As if this were not enough, violence is a multifaceted and multifarious phenomenon with a virtual presence in all spheres, including that of aesthetics. This chapter weighs violence from the perspective of its forms of expression, leaving to the side (or to the field of intervention of this volume's other chapters) another series of approaches that, it is only fair to acknowledge, are at the center of public debate and of greatest interest to the average citizen. However that may be, I do not believe that it is an exaggeration to affirm that some of this study's conclusions may contribute to shedding light on the tangled motives that make violence, in its multiple manifestations, so present in our way of life.

Although this may seem obvious, there is no way to appropriately address violence as an aesthetic phenomenon without drawing a categorical distinction between reality and its representation. Unfortunately, there are many people who experience violent acts or are daily witnesses to them, but fortunately, there are many more people who become acquainted with such acts through what we can refer to as the communications media. From my perspective, violence comes in two genres: real violence, or that which is experienced in situ, and represented violence. In what follows, I will be concerned only with the latter, considering one of its manifestations exclusively. In other words, the pages that follow study the visual representation of violence, taking as a laboratory the teeming and promiscuous aesthetic space known as the audiovisual, a crossroads at which film meets all the forms of expression—from television in its various formats to video art and video games, by way of the variegated universe fostered by cyberspace—that today question its hegemony.

Far from being arbitrary or random, these foundational choices aim to respond to the iconic inflation with regard to violence that is evident in our environment. The fact that violent images bubble up through all the audiovisual windows is food for thought. Undoubtedly, powerful anthropological, historical, cultural, and psychological reasons could be adduced to justify this tendency of humanity toward violence. Everything indicates, nonetheless, that the ubiquity of visual representations of violence is also rooted in a question of symbolic efficacy. In fact, violence today constitutes a captivating spectacle from which we cannot avert our eyes because, among other reasons, human beings have laboriously succeeded in constructing a profuse imaginary, with several figurative registers, in order to manage it for both financial and aesthetic profit. It is possible, in effect, to discern amid today's audiovisual swamp various regimes of visual representation of violence, aesthetic models that will be the center of this chapter's attention.

Some Unrewarding Approaches to the Representation of Violence

Innumerable studies have been published on how violence is expressed, but none addresses the issue from a materialist perspective or, if I may so put it, one centered on the materiality of forms that could support our attempt to map the figuration of violence in use today. For example, the bulk of approaches to the subject limit themselves to evaluating the media coverage of violent events in terms of moral criteria. The massive amounts of ink spilled over the journalistic treatment of violence against women or military conflicts, two of the manifestations of barbarism that have magnetically attracted content analysis aimed at safeguarding political correctness, can serve as an example.

Paying attention to the approach, justification, explications, and descriptions provided by news reports of violent incidents, studies of this kind have meticulously identified the values and attitudes projected by the media. We therefore know that the quantity and quality of news reports varies as a function of the geographic location of the conflict, the geopolitical influence of the opposing factions, and above all, the birthplace of those killed or wounded in combat, in the same way that the formidable visibility of aggression against women in the current news landscape is also a reflection of the industry's commercial opportunism to cash in on the somewhat morbid interest aroused by occurrences of this kind. It should not surprise us that such studies, denouncing the Eurocentric and imperialist and/or patriarchal and androcentric model that also dominates the journalistic imaginary, should generally conclude with a series of recommendations aimed at eradicating uses of news that legitimate stereotypes and dangerous or politically incorrect attitudes.

These evaluative frameworks oriented toward denunciation and redress are also dominant today when it comes time to calibrate the ways in which violence finds a place in audiovisual fiction. Pragmatics, reception theory, postcolonial theory, gender studies, and cultural studies (the epistemological currents that monopolize the academic center of reflection on the audiovisual phenomenon at present) share the idea that "media spectatorship . . . is thus a negotiable site of interaction and struggle, seen, for example, in the possibility of 'aberrant' or resistant readings" (Shohat and Stam 1994, 347). This archipelago of schools, each with its own particular refinements, that addresses the debated subject of interpretation in accordance with national, ethnic, class, gender, or ideological criteria stresses the fact that the spectator's *individual identity characteristics* determine his or her comprehension of the audiovisual text. Using this measuring stick, analyzing the audiovisual representation of violence becomes purely an opinion survey about the ways in which different "interpretive communities"[1] deal ideologically, morally, and emotionally with the act of

---

1. The concept comes from Stanley Fish (1980) and is very similar to the proposition put forward by Stuart Hall, one of the founding fathers of cultural studies, that there are sociologically distinct modes of being a spectator.

barbarism depicted. Reception becomes a discursive battlefield on which the different interpretive subjects seek to reaffirm their identity by undertaking resistant readings, thereby denying any protagonism not only to the materiality of cinematic forms but also, more seriously, to their effects of literal meaning.

As if this were not enough, this epistemological framework has been fertile ground for the concept of *symbolic violence* proposed by Pierre Bourdieu from a sociological perspective.[2] Each looking to his or her own concerns, scholars belonging to these schools have applied Bourdieu's concept to whatever representation (whether it is an act of barbarism or not) turns out to be offensive from the historically, culturally, politically, and/or socially founded perspective of a particular interpretive community. This is the case, for example, of the *Tarzan* and *Rambo* movies, in which viewers' identification with the white hero has been described by these cultural critics as symbolic violence against African and Vietnamese audiences.[3]

Despite their interest, approaches centered on the values and social uses of the visual depiction of violence are of little use for a project like the one proposed here, which aims to develop a taxonomy of its forms and mechanisms of expression, because, as we will see, the tactics for the figuration of barbarism exist per se, independent of the subsequent semantic use or significance they may acquire once inserted into one or another discursive context. In other words, the documentary format, that enunciative apparatus configured around certain specific, formal, easily listable, and classifiable stylemes, can be mobilized without distinction for the purposes of legitimating, banalizing, or denouncing the act of violence shown. These formal traits, like those that characterize the apparatus of fiction, are essentially abstract, signifying functions lacking a priori content and potentially susceptible to becoming the carriers of any possible effect of meaning. They are, consequently, audiovisual notations that are objectively neutral from the semantic perspective, and hence from the ideological one.

---

2. The notion of symbolic violence plays a central role in the general analysis of domination undertaken by Pierre Bourdieu, without which it is impossible to understand the shared roots of phenomena as heterogeneous as colonialism, class-based domination, and men's domination of women. For a language-centered explanation, see Bourdieu (1991).

3. On the instability of cinematographic identification in the *Tarzan* movies, see Frantz Fanon (1967).

In the following section, I will propose an approach that, as Greimasian semiotics would put it, describes those forms that preexist on the figurative level while leaving aside their links to the thematic level. From that perspective, it will then be feasible to sketch a taxonomy of those materials that function today as audiovisual containers for violent content. It is a matter, as I have been suggesting, of a finite catalog of singular forms that are combined according to aesthetic patterns and models, through which, if I may be permitted the expression, the audiovisual inscription of barbarism is brought to the fore.

The Referential Regime and the Transformational Regime

A warning before we begin: there will be no discussion here of the ontology of violent images; their falsehood or truthfulness; whether they are documentary images that mimetically reflect real acts of barbarism or are, on the contrary, apocryphal reconstructions of violent acts staged for that purpose. These issues, of supreme importance in areas such as journalism and the courts, are entirely irrelevant to the subject that concerns us, which is that of the different degrees of verisimilitude and credibility in the visual and aural representation of violent acts. These exist because of the existence, deeply rooted in our subconscious, of a series of symbolic conventions according to which acts of barbarism appear more or less plausible depending on the figurative mechanisms that give them audiovisual form. Bringing to light the foundations of these conventions will help us to elucidate the aesthetic experience of violence.

In essence, the figurative strategies we associate with the documentary genre produce a kind of *truth effect* of represented violence on the viewer, while those that we associate with the fictional sphere foster what we might preliminarily designate as an *art effect*. Although as we will see, conventional identifications of this kind are not always pertinent.

This being the case, we can map out with some precision two major aesthetic spaces or models of inscription counterpoised to each other: the *referential regime* (since it seeks in essence to reproduce the violent act with legitimizing or mimetic aims) and the *transformational regime* (whenever barbarism is taken as an aesthetic object or a pretext for engaging in rhetorical maneuvers).

These two grand axes, which promote antithetical patterns for the representation of violence, manifest internal doublings or divisions in turn, such that in the end, we would seem to have four formal paradigms,

autonomous but related to one another by ties of opposition, contradiction, and complementarity.[4] Let us review them each in turn, with attention to their practical implementation.

The Two Models of Referential Inscription: From the Raw Document to the Forms of Documentary Discourse

One of the unique aspects that made 9/11 into the violent spectacle par
excellence of the twenty-first century so far has to do with its unusual
visibility, with the fact that the attack on the World Trade Center's Twin
Towers occurred in a location with one of the world's highest concentra-
tions of cameras per square foot, precisely at the time of day when Western
television stations are in the habit of broadcasting news programs.[5] As is
well known, they all interrupted their planned news reporting in order to
broadcast, absolutely live, the images of the North Tower in flames and
were doing so when the second plane hit the South Tower, followed by the
eventual vertical collapse of both colossuses.

Despite that fact that those of us who witnessed that event on television may have viewed it as a whole, two referential levels can be distinguished within that discursive object. One corresponds to the iron rules of
that television format that we call "the news," which, over and above each
channel's specific variations, is based on a series of standardized, immediately recognizable stylemes: namely, one or several talking heads seated
behind a table and speaking directly to the camera as they give an account
of certain events; over-the-shoulder (OTS) inserts, where applicable, or
taking over the whole screen, that show images alluding to the facts being
recounted; and the anchor alternating the lead speaking role with another
journalist deployed in situ, as it happens or subsequently. The second
level corresponds to the images and/or sounds that document the incident in the news and that occasionally (as on 9/11) serve as a foundation

---

4. Even if this point cannot be developed here, it should be noted that this four-group organization is inspired by the ideas of Algridas J. Greimas, particularly his notion of the semiotic
square. See Greimas and Courtés (1982).

5. On the U.S. East Coast, the attack coincided with the morning news shows (the first plane
hit at 8:45 a.m. New York time), while in Western Europe, it broke into the day's prime time
for news (2:45 p.m. Central European time), when the midday news services were on the air.
All the details of the attack, including its timing, were planned so as to maximize its potential
visualization.

for and/or endorsement of the talking heads' accounts.[6] As a general rule, these documentary images and/or sounds do not appear in their raw state. Instead they are processed or filtered for informational purposes; that is, they are contextualized within a series of signs and indicators that inscribe the event within an informational account and mark it as a news item.[7] These signs and indicators include, for example, one or more off-camera voices that gloss the images, the logo of the news channel, text alluding to some factual aspect (geographical location and time of the occurrence, name of the person responsible for the documentary recording, and so on), and graphic allusions—of the type "Direct," "On Air," "Breaking News"—intended to attract the viewer's attention. If we were to strip away from the images of the Twin Towers in flames all these codified additions that model them as news[8] and extract them from the discursive structure or audiovisual flow of the provision of news and information, we would have what Santos Zunzunegui in his essay "Tanatorios de la visión" [Funeral homes of vision] (2005, 77–93) calls an "event-image," inverting the terms of Jean Baudrillard's "image-event" concept, and what Olivier Joyard (2001) calls a "zero image," a documentary image in its pure state.

There, in the qualitative leap from the event depicted by the raw document to the narrative reconstruction made from it by the audiovisual format that we call "the news," is where we find the border, no doubt porous and fragile but heuristically valid, that allows us to distinguish the two complementary models of the referential inscription of violence: one that corresponds to the *document* and one that is characteristic of *documentary discourse*. In other words, two figural registers are superimposed in the referential regime: a primary register characteristic of that literal graphic representation that denotes immediacy and absolute transparency with respect to the violent event it reflects, and another, manifestly constructed register that inserts the event into the codified framework of a discourse that aims to narratively explain or process the act of barbarism.

---

6. In the case I am examining here, however, the terms were reversed, since the course of events illustrated by the documentary images was followed only with some difficulty by the off-screen commentary of the presenters.

7. This was taken to an extreme by some U.S. stations that showed the images of the attack on the Twin Towers over banners with labels such as "America under Attack," "America at War," and "America's New War."

8. Often, documentary materials are "domesticated" with an eye to their informational use, altering their materiality by blurring faces, license plates, commercial brands, and so on, or highlighting the parts of the image that are of interest to the story at hand with filters or soft-focus effects.

As is obvious, both referential registers have other standardized codifications beyond the "live" event-image and the news program. On the side of the raw document, we have perfectly recognizable figurative models available such as the home movie, the hidden camera, the surveillance camera, and the "candid camera" practical joke, subformats of documentary texts that, whether due to their banality, rudeness, or impromptu nature, have no place in the informational grids of television daily news but nevertheless proliferate in the blogosphere.[9] In fact, Internet platforms such as YouTube and Myspace[10] have become privileged windows on the unstoppable flood of violent documentary images of all kinds that saturate our audiovisual landscape: arbitrary acts of aggression recorded with cell phone cameras, domestic accidents and brutal robberies captured by surveillance cameras, chance violent occurrences caught on video by passersby or tourists, images of chases and arrests filmed by cameras installed in police cars, incidents of police brutality recorded by hidden precinct cameras, and so on.

Since this list could be extended almost without end, I will point to two emblematic cases that give a precise idea of the aesthetic order of the violent document. The first is what has become known as "jihadi snuff," homemade or amateur videos bearing witness to the terrorist acts perpetrated by Al-Qaeda's mujahideen: bomb attacks filmed from a safe distance, prisoners being shot, hostages beheaded in front of the camera, and so forth.[11] The second is the "Zapruder film," the color images that Abraham Zapruder, perched on a pedestal on the western side of Dealey Plaza with a Bell and Howell eight-millimeter camera at the ready, filmed of the presidential motorcade during the visit made by JFK and his wife, Jacqueline, to Dallas on November 22, 1963. The 26.6-second film (containing a total of 486 frames) shows the U.S. president being struck by the three bullets, the last right to the head, which ended his life. This miniscule fragment of negative constitutes, with equal status to the

---

9. On a closer analysis, one might suggest that the step from violent *incident* to violent *event* is affected by the display format itself: the blogosphere has room for all kinds of violent incidents, while the documentary format only takes account of those that attain the status of an event. Having noted this distinction, I will continue for reasons of convenience to use the concepts without differentiation, as if they were synonyms.

10. Ogiris.com, a website that aggregates uncensored multimedia material on death and violence of all kinds, is the most abysmal example of this state of affairs.

11. We find a sui generis variant in the images of Saddam Hussein's hanging, recorded using a cell phone camera.

conglomerate of images of the Twin Towers attack, the paradigm of the violent documentary image of the twentieth century. Most interesting for our purposes, together with the "jihadi snuff" from which, significantly, it is distinguished by neither formal nor thematic elements, the Zapruder film incarnates the "zero degree" of the raw document.

As far as the other register of the referential regime is concerned, there are other documentary formats or devices in addition to the standard television news program. Some are perfectly codified, such as the historical documentary in which an off-camera voice, speaking over a sequence of images, the majority of which originated as raw documents, fixes a single narrative meaning among all the possible ones;[12] or the televised rebroadcast of sports with a strong violent component, such as martial arts, American football, and boxing.[13] At the same time, there are other formats of a less precise aesthetic geography, such as this promiscuous overarching format that we generically call the "documentary," encompassing everything from televised current-events reporting on war, crime, and other violent occurrences to historical, scientific, and popularizing documentaries that retrospectively reconstruct past violent occurrences.[14]

---

12. For example, *Why We Fight* (1942–1945), the magnificent series of seven propaganda documentaries directed by Frank Capra, with the occasional assistance of Anatol Litvak, during World War II, in which the causes and course of the military campaigns of the largest military conflict in history are narrated at the intellectual level of the average American.

13. Consider the case of the fight between Evander Holyfield and Mike Tyson at the MGM Las Vegas Grand Garden Arena on June 28, 1997, famous because, in addition to the violence inherent in a fight in which the world heavyweight championship was at stake, Tyson bit off part of Holyfield's right ear. The event, which staged the opportunity for revenge after a previous fight in which the all-powerful Tyson lost his crown, was heavily publicized with a campaign that, like a Hollywood launch, announced the fight with the hackneyed title *The Sound and the Fury: Holyfield-Tyson II*. The televised rebroadcast by CBS's Showtime network, with Steve Albert, Ferdie Pacheco, and Bobby Czyz as presenters, reached its zenith when the use of his teeth by the aspirant to the title interrupted the course of the fight, and the broadcast covered the impasse by replaying the moment of bloodshed from every perspective and at every speed imaginable. We see here the extreme case in which the documentary manipulation of a sports rebroadcast subjects the event-image to a process of stylization recalling the stylistic practices that I will later call "mannerist."

14. One good example among thousands might be the first episode, titled "El asesinato de Carrero Blanco" [The murder of Carrero Blanco], of the series *La transición española* [The Spanish transition], produced by RTVE under the direction of Elías Andrés, with a script and narration by Victoria Prego. The segment, first broadcast on July 23, 1995, used a profusion of archival materials and accounts by the era's leading political actors to reconstruct the ETA attack that took the life of the admiral who led the Spanish government. Also in this category are those nature documentaries in which violence plays a starring role: for example, those that depict the hunting tactics of African savanna predators and the way in which they settle the identity of the alpha male.

Neither exhaustive nor as precise as might be hoped, this attempt at classification nonetheless enables us to appreciate with some clarity the practical existence of two perfectly distinguishable figurative registers within the referential regime. It is a matter, in essence, of two kinds of audiovisual calligraphy that lead, along quite distinct and nonetheless complementary aesthetic paths, to the same truth effect, independent—and this is the decisive point—of the ontology of the violent incident they depict. Whether those incidents are true or false, I insist, does not affect the plausibility that the spectator conventionally attributes to those audiovisual inscription models that he or she considers conveyers of truth. In fact, the most effective method will be for us to empty these models of content, retaining solely the formal receptacles, and to inventory the hallmarks of truthfulness that contribute in each case (because a text's plausibility does not depend solely on the presence of these stylemes) to creating that truth effect.

The stylemes that shape the peculiar calligraphy of the raw document are, strictly speaking, ways of *appearing* as a document—that is, significant traits that denote spontaneity, neutrality, and/or improvisation, the antithesis, if you will, of the effort to figuratively domesticate the violence denoted by the remainder of the aesthetic formats that we will be reviewing. I am referring to a series of *analogical indicators* or iconic engines of veracity that transgress in some way the format of professional inscription. To summarize quickly (and it is obvious that this inventory needs considerable refinement), the calligraphy of the document institutes a sort of aesthetics of the random or the fortuitous, impugning in two ways the professional standards that we associate with formal elaboration, or with stylization seeking an aesthetic effect.[15]

First, by way of *emphasis on the material foundation,* a space that encompasses all the sensory indicators that denote the mediation of a substandard technology: graininess, color imbalance, black and white without contrasts, poor focus, abrupt or random use of zoom, little depth of field, poor, excessive, or badly directed light, the use of night-vision or infrared cameras, jumped frames,[16] and so on.

---

15. Even if, as I will indicate later on, formal elaboration may be directed toward imitating this kind of inscription.

16. Surveillance cameras indiscriminately photograph whatever passes in front of them, but in order to save film, they do so at a rate below the twenty-four or twenty-five images per second that produce the perfect illusion of movement on our retina. The result is a sequence in which objects and people move by fits and starts.

Second, by way of *planning,* through which all those traits (and the typology is certainly extensive) come together and connote an amateur, neutral, or improvised visual depiction, in which perspective, distance, and camera movement are, generically speaking, inappropriate or counterproductive for the clear visualization of the violent act shown. A series of indicators contribute to this effect: for example, that the camera was placed prior to the incident recorded;[17] that it is too far from or too close to the event; that the focus is off; that the camera's movements, whether its imperturbable motionlessness that leaves the action sporadically outside its view or the abrupt changes of position it undergoes in its eagerness to record that action, disfigure its transparent representation of the event; that an editorial hand is glaringly absent or intervenes abruptly; or that the flow of images concludes before the action does.

This substandard visual morphology that characterizes the aesthetic of the fortuitous has its audio equivalent in a series of acoustic markers or indicators that contravene the standards of professional quality: poor equalization; cacophonous effects; conversations that are scarcely audible or tangled in background noise; voices filtered through other technological devices such as the telephone, a megaphone, or emergency radios.

Drawing up a taxonomy of the forms of documentary discourse is more complex, since it is an amalgam or archformat that, as we have already said, is organized into various relatively codified and autonomous subformats. Since my aim is not to carry out an exhaustive classification of the stylemes that make up documentary inscription or the documentary figurative registry, but rather to call attention to their existence and possible praxis, it may perhaps be sufficient to lay out some of the verifying hallmarks that define and distinguish documentary discourse from the raw document: the mechanisms, in sum, that produce a truth effect in synergy with that audiovisual dirtiness that, as we have just indicated, functions as an analogical indicator for the documentary image.

For this purpose, we will use the case of the investigative report titled *11-S, un asunto envenenado* (distributed in English as *Toxic Affair of 9/11*), a documentary produced by the French firm GAD and directed by Xavier Deleau that addresses, eight years after the fact, the serious aftereffects that the recovery and demolition work has had for those who were at Ground Zero. To this end, it combines archival footage of the day of the attack and

---

17. The paradigmatic case is that of the surveillance camera's hieratic eye, which has given rise to the "fly-on-the-wall" style of documentary production.

the recovery and cleanup work that followed with personal testimonies by the protagonists and their families, as well as statements by doctors and experts who have been treating those affected by dust inhaled at the World Trade Center. Over that visual track, a narrator's voice weaves the elements together, explaining the facts; organizing the sequence of speakers; and denouncing the negligent behavior of the authorities, who gave assurances at the time that the dust was essentially innocuous and later washed their hands ominously of those affected, some of whom are today without health insurance and nearly indigent.

Without going into greater detail, we can observe that this kind of documentary reporting's apparatus is characterized grosso modo by a precise dialectic between the visual track and the sound, in which the off-screen voice traces the thread of the discourse and the image endorses it, via the alternation (this cutting back and forth becomes the key syntactic figure) between the past (made manifest in documentary images that have undergone a greater or lesser degree of processing) and the present (retrospective accounts that remember the past episode). Another characteristic is the film's ambivalent audiovisual physiognomy, such that the fragments marked by the archival material's substandard quality coexist with numerous scenes of present-day speakers filmed with great polish (some of them amid idyllic landscapes that contrast with the disastrous "prop" of Ground Zero). Broadly sketched, these can be understood as the identifying marks of one of the formats adopted by documentary inscription, conventionally considered by the spectator a vehicle for true facts.

Nevertheless, anyone minimally acquainted with contemporary culture will know that this presumption has been called into question by a certain kind of fictional film that has vampirized the various stylistic markers of the referential regime. Examples are everywhere, but I believe that none is a more conclusive demonstration of the profitable results of transporting the historical documentary's discursive forms to the terrain of fiction than *Zelig* (1983), a film in which Woody Allen, by way of a cinematic device that mimics the formal resources of the documentary, narrates the incredible adventures of an individual whose body can transform into the appearance of others.[18] Nor does there exist a more insightful and exhaustive catalog of the different formal variants adopted today by the substandard inscription of the raw document than Brian de Palma's *Redacted*

---

18. The essence of the film rests in the idea that both the protagonist and the story of his life are chameleonlike insofar as they acquire the external aspect of what they are not.

(2007), a film based on bloody, real incidents that took place in Iraq but that situates itself unambiguously in fictional territory. To continue with the same topic, the American presence in Iraq has recently provided the basis for *Green Zone* (2010), by Paul Greengrass, a fictional film impregnated with violence that in its formal elements adopts without hesitation the handheld camera footage, the forced out-of-focus images, and the convulsive editing that we have attributed to the raw document's impure calligraphy. Along the same lines, but with very different plot materials, films such as *The Blair Witch Project* (1999), by Daniel Myrick and Eduardo Sánchez, the concept of which was imitated by Jaume Balagueró and Paco Plaza in *Rec* (2007),[19] appear as fictional fragments of the hazy aesthetic applied to assorted histories bathed in blood and violence.

The profitability of measuring textual objects with attention to their discursive effects, instead of in terms of truth, can be appreciated in contexts like this one. In all the cases mentioned in the preceding paragraph, the aesthetic effect or impact of the referential regime's distinctive formal traits takes priority over the verisimilitude that, by inertia, they confer on fictional narrative. The document's convulsive calligraphy and the documentary apparatus are, in all the cases just considered, aesthetic arguments or motifs more than they are marks of truthfulness. The visual characteristics of the handheld camera and abrupt editing, for example, prevail over their power to convince. Their stylization and ornamental use, in sum, locate them on the other side of the playing field from the figurative model that I have earlier called the transformational regime. It will therefore be useful to specify without further delay the traits that define that model as the antonym of the referential regime and to make clear the forms and mechanisms of expression that characterize it.

Allusive and/or Elusive Stylization[20]

There is no effective way to calibrate the transformational regime (the one that takes violence as an excuse or aesthetic object) without taking into account what the English poet Samuel Taylor Coleridge (1907, chap. 14) called "willing suspension of disbelief," on which narrative fiction is founded. The audiovisual stylization of violent acts can be comfortably

---

19. In addition, the Spanish film presents itself as if it were a live broadcast by a television news service, thus locating this alleged document in the documentary field.

20. The terms are equally appropriate, as we will see, given that the aesthetic maneuver consists in *eluding* the depiction of the violent act in order to rhetorically *allude* to it .

situated in that discursive territory, in which the model spectator accepts the premises on which the fiction is based, despite being aware of their falsity, in order to enjoy the pleasures of the text. Under the umbrella of this weak credulity, the spectator assumes that the violence he or she is shown is, like the totality of the discourse that contains it, laboriously constructed for his or her viewing pleasure. The transformational regime, in sum, modifies, retouches, adorns, and embellishes violence for aesthetic purposes.

The audiovisual stylization of violence can take place by way of the implementation of extremely heterogeneous figurative strategies. It does not seem too far a stretch, nevertheless, to maintain that this formal elaboration aimed at the visual depiction of violence can be generically resolved in two ways: by means of elusive stylization or by means of mannerist stylization. In other words, when it comes time to visually manage the figure of the violent, we have two stylization modes available, one that pivots around what is not seen, the other around what is seen. Let us begin with the former.

We have indicated that the documentary arch format has the objective of explaining the violent event in detail, approaching it from all angles, including its explicit exhibition by means of the manipulation of documentary images, should they exist, or their processing as "news." Elusive stylization, conversely, instead of showing the violent event explicitly, seeks to produce a sinuous aesthetic effect by a web of allusions to it.[21] From this we see that elusive stylization is the opposite pole or the antithesis of the documentary apparatus.

To synthesize, elusive stylization has historically been put to use by filmmakers who are convinced that the potential of a medium of expression that visually depicts the world is not exhausted by what is explicitly shown, but rather, on the contrary, could be greatly strengthened by the contribution of the space outside the frame, as well as the various tactics that present dramatic incidents obliquely or in parable form. For obvious

---

21. Even if only in a footnote, it must be emphasized that elusive stylization attains its chemically pure formulation in those cases in which the camera leaves the violent act out of the frame, in order to show in its place an adjacent neutral space in which that violence has no visible impact whatsoever. From Jean Renoir (*Le bête humaine*, 1938) to Charles Chaplin (*Monsieur Verdoux*, 1947) by way of John Ford (*The Searchers*, 1956), some of history's greatest filmmakers have occasionally opted to avoid the direct depiction of barbarism. This "zero degree" of elusive stylization, as we will see shortly, allows distinct modalities (metonymic or metaphorical) of rhetorical projection.

reasons, violence has been, together with sex and the monstrous, one of the thematic motifs that have contributed most generously to the development of that kind of *poetics of the implicit*, on which the figurative tactics of elusive stylization are based. While the casuistry is very extensive and heterogeneous, I find that, in practice, there are two generic procedures for alluding to violence that has been confined or displaced outside the frame—that is, two rhetorical formulas for elusive stylization—metonymy and metaphor.

The rhetorical figure of metonymy, as is well known, has various manifestations, some of which can help us to shed light on the nature of that allusive stylization that diverts the spectator's gaze from the act of barbarism. The mechanism of synecdoche (alluding to a whole by means of one of its parts), for example, is at the conceptual origin of the stylizing maneuvers that leave the violent act in the off-screen space contiguous to the camera frame, in order to give an oblique account of it with the irruption into the frame of some of its elements, whether the noise created, the shadow projected, the blood spattered, or the damage caused in the immediate vicinity. Also essentially metonymic is that stylizing tactic that eludes violence's direct depiction for the purpose of alluding to it by showing its impact or effects on the characters who, unlike the spectator, see it. Likewise metonymic is that magnificent cinematographic idea that consists in evading the crude exhibition of barbarism by means of a character's verbal gloss.

Since the examples are once again legion, I will only point out one, which in addition to being definitive, functions as a vade mecum for all the tactics of metonymic stylization just identified. *Cat People* (1942) tells the improbable story of Irena Dubrovna, a beautiful young woman who turns into a panther and kills a man. Driven by a very tight budget, Val Lewton and Jacques Tourneur, the film's producer and director, respectively, opted to suggest the feline and her ravages rather than show them, to which end they made use of the shadows, noises, traces, and collateral damage resulting from her violent outbursts with such efficacy and brilliance that this RKO B movie is considered one of the gems of classic American film. Inevitably, one of its climactic moments takes places at the end of the film, when the young woman, transformed into a beast, attacks her psychiatrist and kills him in an unequal physical combat that is resolved metonymically, by means of the stylized shadows projected onto the wall by a fallen lamp[22] as well as by the heartrending sounds of the fight. By this point, the spectator knows that the young woman's prodigious shape-shifting ability is owed to certain bloody incidents that occurred in her family and made her the victim of a fatal curse (her mother apparently killed her father). Now, those gruesome events, instead of being visually depicted in the usual form of a flashback, are mentioned by the psychiatrist following a hypnosis session in which the young woman seems to have made frequent allusion to the "primal scene." The film, to conclude, has two masterful scenes (the pool scene and the one that takes place in the studio where Irena's husband works), in which, in addition to the shadows and roars of the beast, the reactions of terror by the individuals who see the panther on the prowl with the worst of intentions become the metonymic projection screen of a latent violence that does not become visible.

The metaphorical variant of elusive stylization, for its part, consists in replacing direct depiction of the violent act with the presentation of an image to which it has a certain similarity or that represents the act of barbarism in parable form, by means of an image that evokes it symbolically. Metaphorical elusion has not borne such vast fruits as the metonymic version, but we have some dazzling examples that bear witness to its potential. Let one taken from halfway around the world suffice.

In *Genroku chushingura* (1941–1942), Kenji Mizoguchi tells a story that is so well known[23] that it enables him to narrate against the background of what is already known, declining to show some of the dramatic plot links, of which the spectator, who already knows the details, is informed indirectly through maneuvers of pure metonymic stylization: by way of a verbal gloss (the neuralgic event of the plan for revenge—that is, the assault on the castle by Oishi's men and the death of the infamous Kira—is recounted secondhand through a letter read by the maidservant of their deceased chieftain Asano's widow) or thanks to off-screen sounds (the climatic final scene leaves out of view the successive *seppuku* of the forty-seven samurai, revealed to us only by the chanting of their names, declaimed by the sacrificial rite's officiant). This entire bloodbath, and the story as a whole, has its origin in Asano's inaugural *seppuku,* which, omit-

---

22. For a more detailed description of the role played by shadows in this peerless film and in others of similar excellence, see Santos Zunzunegui (2009).

23. Not only to a Japanese audience: Jorge Luis Borges, for example, narrated it five years earlier in *El incivil maestro de ceremonias Kotsuké no Suké* [The Insulting Master of Etiquette Kôtsuké no Suké], collected in *Historia universal de la infamia* [A Universal History of Infamy] (1935; English translation, 1972).

ted de facto, is illustrated in parable form through the metaphorical image of his wife cutting off her long hair in rigorous synchronicity with the act that leads to her widowhood and ultimately unleashes the massacre.

Mannerist Stylization

Despite the fertile resources of rhetorical elision, the central ring of the iconic circus of violence is to be found today in the mannerist stylization sphere. All aspects of the contemporary audiovisual, from film in its various genres[24] to video games, by way of fictional television programs and video art, have made explicit violence an element of all kinds of refined stylistic exercises. If rhetorical elision dodges the direct depiction of barbarism with a view to aesthetic effect, mannerist stylization, its logical complement, scrutinizes it for the identical purpose.[25] If the raw document captures the instantaneous blaze of violence, without intermediaries, mannerist stylization, its logical opposite, stages it with a jeweler's precision, underlining its aesthetic values.[26]

The very famous shower scene in Alfred Hitchcock's *Psycho* (1960) can serve as a paradigm case, since in it the three characteristics that define the mannerist stylization of violence are present: its explicit nature (the violence is depicted absolutely front and center), its vocation as a stylistic exercise (demonstrated in this case through the editing techniques), and its tendency to immoderation and excess. On the basis of these three pillars, the praxis of mannerist stylization has evolved like a spreading weed to the point of smothering today's iconic landscape.

Despite the fact that this study is already long enough, I cannot resist mentioning a few archetypal examples. In addition to the tactics of fragmentation tried out by Hitchcock in *Psycho,* other more or less standardized figurative mechanisms exist for the formal declension of violence. I am thinking, for example, about the slow-motion footage that became a

---

24. Action movies, thrillers, fantasy and horror, war and martial-arts movies, science fiction, and even historical films are inconceivable today without the mannerist stylization of violence.

25. The differences between the two are immediately obvious if we compare Kenji Mizoguchi's ellipsis of the taking of the castle in *Genroku chushingura* to the expansive visual symphonies composed by Akira Kurosawa in the battles of *Kumonosu-Ju* (1957), *Kagemusha* (1980), and *Ran* (1985).

26. The qualitative leap between the raw document and mannerist stylization becomes evident if we compare the Zapruder film to the meticulous reconstruction of the assassination by Oliver Stone in *JFK* (1991), made by juxtaposing archival images—including the Zapruder material—with all kinds of images created ad hoc.

hallmark of Sam Peckinpah's violence-soaked films. The technique's lat-
est technological descendant is the "bullet-time fighting" used with such
abandon by the Wachowski brothers in the *Matrix* trilogy (1999–2003).
This also applies to the grotesque theatricalism that characterizes "splat-
ter" or "gore" movies, a subgenre of the horror film identified by graphic
violence, an excess of hemoglobin, and mutilations. Another of these elements is the choreographic stylization of violence, which finds its maximum exponent in that martial-arts genre that, after thriving for years in
the B-movie market, has made the leap to Hollywood's blockbuster bud-
gets. I should also add, even on a very narrow definition, the performative
variant of this model employed in video games, in which the most outra-
geous violence is produced interactively with the spectator.

This profusion of figurative registers exhibiting the mannerist stylization of barbarism has left memorable iconographic traces in the contemporary audiovisual field. The battles waged on celluloid, the anthology
of which was created by filmmakers such as S. M. Eisenstein (*Alexander
Nevsky*, 1935), Orson Welles (*Chimes at Midnight*, 1965), Akira Kurosawa (*Ran*, 1985), Steven Spielberg (*Saving Private Ryan*, 1998), and Peter
Jackson (the *Lord of the Rings* trilogy, 2001–2003), have cast the pictorial
legacy of battle into the shade. Today's action-movie fight scenes, cho-
reographed by the most renowned specialists,[27] are worthy equals to the
song-and-dance numbers of classic Hollywood's greatest musicals. After
developing on a lesser scale in Hong Kong and Taiwan, that exponential levitation of the martial-arts movie known as the *wuxia* genre has
attained in the hands of Ang Lee (*Crouching Tiger, Hidden Dragon*, 2002)
and above all Zhang Yimou[28] a splendor that leaves its literary origins in
the dust. Even the most optimistic diagnosis must recognize, however,
that these are islands of beauty surrounded by a sea of mud, the strident
violence of most productions.

---

27. For example, the *Bourne Trilogy* (2002–2007), especially its last two installments directed
by Paul Greengrass, in which the striking hand-to-hand combats were so successfully choreo-
graphed by the prestigious Jeff Imada that he became sought after as a motion-capture actor for
Xbox and PlayStation video games.

28. Ching Siu-Tung's choreography and Zhang Yimou's direction make the trilogy composed
of *Hero* (2002), *House of Flying Daggers* (2004), and *Curse of the Golden Flower* (2006) a clear
exponent of the beautiful textures offered by stylized violence.

By Way of Conclusion

We may conclude by recalling the central idea of this text that the formidable visibility of violence in our iconosphere is owed in large part to an "effectiveness of symbols" question.[29] We have available, in effect, four major, fully operational models for the audiovisual management of barbarism. On the one hand, we find the raw document and the documentary arch format, the two complementary figurative registers that propose themselves as mimetic reflections of the violent incident. On the other hand are allusive stylization and mannerist stylization, the two sides of the coin that consist in taking barbarism as an aesthetic object or a pretext for rhetorical maneuvers. As if this were not enough, these four figurative archetypes cross-pollinate one another,[30] with the result that violence today has become a fascinating spectacle that has enchanted our gaze.

References

Borges, Jorge Luis. 1972. "The Insulting Master of Etiquette Kôtsuké no Suké." In *A Universal History of Infamy*. Translated by Norman Thomas di Giovanni. New York: Dutton.

Bourdieu, Pierre. 1991. *Language and Symbolic Power*. Translated by Gino Raymond and Mathew Adamson. Edited and introduced by John B. Thompson. Cambridge, MA: Harvard University Press.

Coleridge, Samuel Taylor. 1907. *Biographia literaria*. Oxford: Clarendon Press. Press. First published 1817.

Fanon, Frantz. 1967. *Black Skin, White Masks*. Translated by Charles Markmann. New York: Grove Press.

Fish, Stanley. 1980. *Is There a Text in This Class? The Authority of Interpretive Communities*. Cambridge, MA: Harvard University Press.

Greimas, Algridas J., and Joseph Courtés. 1982. *Semiotics and Language: An Analytical Dictionary*. Translated by Larry Christ, Daniel Patte,

---

29. The idea comes from Claude Lévi-Strauss (1963–1976, chap. 10), who uses it to refer to the healing techniques of shamans and witch doctors, who by manipulating ideas by means of symbols reach a point at which a given situation becomes thinkable and acceptable for the patient and the community. In our context, images and sounds are the materials manipulated with a view toward making represented violence thinkable and acceptable.

30. Boxing matches, as we have already noted, are rebroadcast with slow-motion replays, repeats, and freeze-frame shots that have their origins in mannerist stylization, in the same way that war movies imitate the impure calligraphy of the raw document.

James Lee, Edward McMahon II, Gary Phillips, and Michael Reng-storf. Bloomington: Indiana University Press.

Joyard, Olivier. 2001. "11 Septembre, image zero." *Cahiers du Cinéma* 561 (October): 45.

Lévi-Strauss, Claude. 1963–1976. *Structural Anthropology*. Translated by Claire Jacobson and Brooke Grundfest Schoepf. New York: Basic Books.

Shohat, Ella, and Robert Stam. 1994. *Unthinking Eurocentrism: Multiculturalism and the Media*. London: Routledge.

Zunzunegui, Santos. 2005. *Las cosas de la vida: Lecciones de semiótica estructural*. Madrid: Biblioteca Nueva.

———. 2009. "Sonata de espectros." In *La sombra*, edited by Victor I. Stoichia. Madrid: Museo Thyssen-Bornemisza and Fundación Caja Madrid.

2

The Construction of the Stranger and Social Violence

IMANOL ZUBERO

Translated by Cameron J. Watson

> I was so confident about being a German, a European, a twentieth-century man. Blood? Racial hatred? Not today, not here—at the centre of Europe!
>
> —Victor Klemperer

What Was There before Violence?

José Sanmartín, director of the Reina Sofía Center for the Study of Violence, reminds us of the need to distinguish between aggressiveness and violence, terms that even if they are typically used synonymously, in reality are not: "The former is an innate conduct that is displayed automatically in the face of certain stimuli and inhibited in the face of others. Violence, in contrast, is an intentional more than automatic conduct that can do harm, in other words, which is deliberate aggressiveness" (Sanmartín 2008). We speak about violence as a *deliberate* conduct—deliberate in all senses of the word: intentional, thought about for some time, discussed with others, socialized, accepted, and planned.

Violence begins before, on some occasions long before, it is expressed in the form of aggression. The Yugoslavian Bosnian writer Ivo Andrić knows a lot about this. In his novel *The Bridge on the Drina* he writes:

After the first years of distrust, misunderstanding and hesitation, when the first feeling of transience had passed, the town began to find its place in the new order of things. The people found order, work and security. That was enough to ensure that here too life, outward life at least, set out "on the road of perfection and progress." Everything else was flushed away into that dark background of consciousness where live and ferment the basic feelings and indestructible beliefs of individual races, faiths and castes, which, to all appearances dead and buried, are preparing for later far-off times unsuspected changes and catastrophes without which, it seems, people cannot exist and above all the peoples of this land. (1959, 173–74)

In contrast to what occurs in the case of aggression, before violence there is always deliberation. And the basic result of that deliberation, a result without which violence would remain relegated to that second dark level of consciousness, is always an operation of alienation.

Us and Them

Social violence, collective organized violence, is always the result of an action that has something to do with boundaries. A boundary is drawn up, a dividing line is defined, "we" are distinguished from "them," and then that boundary is transgressed, "their" space is taken over in search of expelling or eliminating them. And this is so easy—so tragically easy to do!

There is an excellent book by the journalist Jean Hatzfeld, *Machete Season*, which is a compilation of conversations he had with some of the Hutus jailed for participating in the killings that, between April and June 1994, led to the deaths of eight hundred thousand Tutsis. One of his observations is especially interesting:

After the genocide, many foreigners wondered how the huge number of Hutu killers recognized their Tutsi victims in the upheaval of the massacres, since Rwandans of both ethnic groups speak the same language with no distinctive differences, live in the same places, and are not always physically recognizable by distinctive characteristics.

The answer is simple. The killers did not have to pick out their victims: they knew them personally. Everyone knows everything in a village. (Hatzfeld 2005, 66)

In effect, they were neighbors massacring neighbors; neighbors who had lived together peacefully for years; neighbors who, from one day to another, stopped doing so, as one of those interviewed by Hatzfeld (2005, 23–24) confessed: "The first person, I finished him off in a rush, not thinking anything of it, even though he was a neighbor, quite close on my hill." He continued: "In truth, it came to me only afterward: I had taken the life of a neighbor. I mean, at the fatal instant I did not see in him what he had been before; I struck someone who was no longer either close or strange to me, who wasn't exactly ordinary anymore, I'm saying like the people you meet every day. His features were indeed similar to those of the person I knew, but nothing firmly reminded me that I had lived beside him for a long time" (Hatzfeld 2005, 24).

Rwanda was, as Hatzfeld points out, a genocide of closeness. In reality, aren't they all? "Murderers quite often seek the proximity of their victims. It is a pious error to suppose that a natural inhibition prevents people from attacking those who are close to them, and recommend intensive one-to-one meetings between criminals and their victims. . . . Proximity rather than anonymity incites people to their worst deeds. Far from raising the threshold of inhibition against violence, it heightens the neighbourly spirit of cruelty" (Sofsky 2003, 165). Genocide and civil war are the most terrible refutation of the so-called contact hypothesis, according to which the mere experience of diversity reinforces ethnic tolerance and social solidarity. Insofar as we interact with people who are not like us, one would hope we gradually overcome our initial doubts and ignorance to ultimately trust them more. Samuel A. Stouffer's classic study, *The American Soldier* (1949), about US soldiers who fought in World War II, concludes that those who served alongside African American troops were more favorable to racial integration than those who did not. This serves as a canonical example of a very seductive perspective for progressively inclined people. Yet things are not as simple as that (Zubero 2010).

It is startling to read *Neighbors* (2001), a book by Jan T. Gross that relates the brutal extermination of the Jewish community in the Polish town of Jedwabne, a small settlement of fewer than three thousand inhabitants of which half were Jewish. On July 10, 1941, 1,600 people, including men, women, and children—almost the entire Jewish population—were massacred by their Catholic neighbors: stoned, beaten, hacked to death, or burned alive. "In Jedwabne," writes Gross:

ordinary Poles slaughtered the Jews. . . . They were men of all ages and of different professions; entire families on occasion, fathers and sons acting in concert; good citizens, one is tempted to say (if sarcasm were not out of place, given the hideousness of their deeds), who heeded the call of municipal authorities. And what the Jews saw, to their horror and, I dare say, incomprehension, were familiar faces. Not anonymous men in uniform, cogs in a war machines, agents carrying out orders, but their own neighbors, who chose to kill and were engaged in a bloody pogrom—willing executioners. (2001, 120–21)

Sixteen hundred people were brutally murdered by their own neighbors—not by anonymous soldiers, not ambushed by criminals, but by normal men with familiar faces: Jakub Kac, stoned to death by Bolek Tamutowski; Eliasz Krawiecki, beaten to death by Czeslaw Laciecz; and so on. Only seven people survived from among the entire Jewish population of Jedwabne. They were spared because there was one family, the Wyrzykowski family, who did not want to participate in the town's horrendous slaughter. Consequently, the Wyrzykowskis opened their doors to Jews fleeing the persecution. They were the only people to do this, the only ones to resist the wave of barbarity that overcame their fellow townspeople.

Violence Washes Whiter

"Great crimes often start from great ideas. . . . Among this class of ideas, pride of place belongs to the vision of purity" (Bauman 1997, 5). The notion of purity, the aspiration for coherence, the desire for identity, and the search for harmony: these are all great ideas that have historically encouraged great horrors. As Bernard-Henri Lévy (1996, 101) points out, "One day a book will have to be written about the desire for purity and how this always produces, everywhere, the same murderous sequence." Building a clean, transparent, predictable, and orderly world is a characteristic aspiration of modernity, an aspiration that one can see at the root of all (the not-infrequent) cases of modern genocide.

The dream of purity is the dream of the natural order of things; it is the aspiration to construct a definitive order, eliminating anything that introduces or sustains a threat to our securities. At its root are uncertainty, chance, conflict, and division, and among all these, the main threat to our security stems from the stranger. The stranger is anyone or anything that does not fit into our cognitive, moral, or aesthetic map of the world (Bauman 1997, 5). But not fitting in like this has an extremely strong and absolute sense. It does not refer to a problem of interpretation, of understanding, as might be the case on so many occasions regarding foreigners' customs or lifestyles. Foreigners have their own place, even though it is not ours; yet what characterizes strangers is that they appear in places they should not: "The opposite of purity—the dirt, the filth, 'polluting agents'—are things 'out of place'" (Bauman 1997, 6).

For that reason the category of stranger is different from that of foreigner, although we might frequently use them synonymously. "There are natives and foreigners, friends and enemies—and there are strangers who do not categorically fit into this model, who dodge, obstruct, and irritate oppositions" (Beck 1998, 127). As Georg Simmel points out in a classic work, the stranger is someone not from elsewhere but from within; he or she is a member of the group itself, and takes on the nature of a real enemy within (Simmel 1950). The stranger is a person physically close to us who we refuse to recognize as a fellow human being or neighbor. Our problem, then, is not that of foreigners who continue to be so even when they live among us (tourists or "guest workers")—unlike those foreigners who adopt, because they want to and can, our ways and rules (sports stars or naturalized artists)—but, rather, those others who live among us without ceasing to be (because they do not want to or, almost always, because they cannot) "others."

"Why does the existence of others bother us?" asks Roger-Pol Droit. "Because they are capable of wanting something different from the predictable and accepted" (2009, 58). The appearance of the other "shatters the rock on which the security of daily life rests" (Bauman 1997, 10). A proliferation of lifestyles threatens the stability of our own convictions and assumptions, on which we build our own existence. It is for that reason that, for most people, culturally diverse situations generate confusion and insecurity.

There are those who adapt well to a scenario in which multiple interpretations of the world coexist. They are the "virtuosos of pluralism" (Berger and Luckmann 1995, 41). Many of them subscribe to an idea expressed some years ago by Félix de Azúa: "Yes, identity kills us, especially because globalized people appear to enjoy a life free of melancholy, nostalgia, or guilt. Like foreigners on vacation in the world" (*El País*, January 5, 2000). Tourists are practitioners of banal cosmopolitanism (Beck 2004; Thorup 2006), a paradigm of the postmodern individual liberated from any kind of connection or commitment (Bauman 1997, chap. 6).

They are nomadic, modern individuals: free human beings, covered in wealth and riches, thirsty for knowledge; nomads because the objects they possess or desire are portable; nomads because of both their work and their consumption (Attali 1991, 87–89). Yet what of most of humanity? For the majority, experiencing cultural diversity becomes an experience of exile, constitutive of modern existence (Nancy 1996). Literally desolate—in other words, deprived of ground—most people see themselves thus deprived of everything that defines them as people: belonging to a social and political community (Finkielkraut 2001, 122). This is the breeding ground for developing identity movements because, as in the first response to Auschwitz survivor Jean Améry's self-imposed question about "how much home a person needs," "all the more, the less of it he can carry with him" (1980, 44). This is at the root of the, at times, ferocious defense of a culturally homogenous and pure territory, free of contamination by the stranger.

There is a directly proportionate relation between the intensity of wishing to reach a state of purity and the capacity to point out elements of impurity in reality—impure realities characterized as obstacles to overcome on the way to achieving the ideal of coherence. In a similar way to anorexia—perhaps the most modern of illnesses, to the extent that it only exists in highly modernized societies—whoever aspires to an ideal of purity will never be satisfied. The more we aspire to coherence, the more we find signs of incoherence. The more we clean, the more dirt we find. The gaze of purity on reality does not cease to find elements that do not fit its ideal. This incessantly uncomfortable gaze lies at the root of what Arjun Appadurai terms the anxiety of incompleteness (2006, 8). And this anxiety is the unstoppable energy that drives the construction of predatory identities that insist on the extinction of those other social categories classified as strange; this almost always coincides with majority identities that see in minorities an unacceptable and permanent reminder of their impossibility to constitute themselves as a homogeneous totality (Appadurai 2006, 51–52).

Basically, we face a totalitarian temptation: the most characteristic feature of totalitarian thought is that it "gives no legitimate place to otherness and plurality" (Todorov 2003, 34–35). Our notion of order is deeply conservative. Order is synonymous with stability, harmony, and especially permanence. From this stems the negative vision of difference, rejected as an intrusion that threatens the stability and permanence of social systems. "Ordering—maintains Bauman—means making reality different than it is, getting rid of the ingredients of reality which are deemed to be responsible for 'impurity,' 'opacity,' 'contingency' of human condition. Once that road has been entered, one may arrive sooner or later at a verdict that some people be refused help, thrown out or destroyed in the name of a 'greater good' and somebody else's 'greater happiness'" (Bauman and Tester 2001, 58). When strategies of normalizing the other fail, when his or her otherness turns out to be irreducible, the only way out is his or her disappearance. When he or she cannot be integrated by means of any reduction, the only recourse is elimination: "There are . . . things for which the 'right place' has not been reserved in any fragment of man-made order. They are 'out of place' everywhere. . . . It won't be enough to move them to another place; one needs to get rid of them once and for all" (Bauman 1997, 6). For that reason, there is just one step from an aspiration to purity to the compulsive practice of (ethnic) cleansing.

From Otherness to Violence

Ethnic cleansing, the elimination of difference, is only possible on the ruins of a community built on mutual acceptance. The elimination of the other demands an ambitious and complex program of disconnecting and, consequently, not taking responsibility. In 1935, a Berlin rabbi described the condition of Jews in Germany in these terms: "Perhaps this has never before happened in the world, and no one knows how long it can be borne; life without a neighbour" (quoted in Bauman 2000, 123). As Bauman points out, the Holocaust was possible only after a long process of the *social production of distance*, a prior condition for the social production of moral indifference. It was only therefore possible to generalize among Germans a conviction that however atrocious the things happening to the Jews were, they had nothing to do with the rest of the population, and consequently no one but the Jews should have to worry about them. Beck, meanwhile, uses the term *political construction of the stranger* to describe the process that converted so many people "from neighbors into Jews," people who were subsequently expelled in practice from the space of rights and responsibilities (Beck 1996, 378–96; 1995, ch. 10). Combining both perspectives, one can thus represent the process that leads to such social violence as a continuum that transitions from otherness, to social distancing, to moral indifference, to social violence.

As regards the experience of concentration camp prisoners when, for different reasons (transfers, work in the cities, and so on), they came into contact with German people, Robert Gellately writes that "although we hear from survivors of help and comfort they received, the overwhelming impression is that Germans were at best indifferent and fearful, and at worst they shared the guards' scorn, hostility, and hatred" (2001, 204).

The same thing happened at the end of the war during the liberation of the camps:

> Citizens on the outside did not rush to help the camp prisoners during their evacuations. There were occasional offers of food and water, there were gestures of sympathy, and even the odd protest about the brutality of the SS or other guards. For the most part, however, good citizens did nothing, either out of fear for their own lives, or because they had grown apathetic or indifferent. (Gellately 2001, 251)

In the words of Mark Mazower: "Most Germans appear to have accepted that Jews were not longer part of their community" (1999, 173).

For his part, Peter Fritzsche (2009, 264) recalls, "Most Germans probably objected to the deportation of their Jewish neighbors, but that opposition was overlaid by the emergence of the abstract image of the Jew as a monolithic, dangerous force precisely at the moment when military setbacks and bombing raids began to preoccupy German thoughts. The effect was growing indifference to the fate of the Jews." The deliberate attitude of ignoring the specific individual in order to see only the category of "Jew,"[1] from another abstraction like "Germany" or "the Germans," was really the starting point of all violence against the Jews:

> Anti-Semitism did not arrive on the scene as something completely new, but it acquired much greater symbolic value when people associated it with being German. The desire to embrace the project of national revival, to convert, to undo Versailles and 1918, helps explain why, often from one day to the next, both prominent and obscure Germans decided for themselves to become consistent in their relations with "the Jews." It was "her duty as a German" to see things from a racial point of view that impelled one acquaintance not long after the Nazis came to power to cut off contact with Victor Klemperer. Intellectuals such as the philosopher

---

1. As Imre Kertész, winner of the Nobel Prize for Literature in 2002, points out: "Jew is that person about whom one can speak in plural, which is how Jews usually are, whose characteristics can be reduced to an essence, like those of a not very complex animal species" (2002, 73).

Martin Heidegger and the jurist Carl Schmidt did the same thing. They simply refused to deal with Jews. (Fritzsche 2009, 121)

It was not anti-Semitism, which had existed prior to the Nazis, that was new in Germany but "the termination of ambiguous, indeterminate social relations among neighbors" (Fritzsche 2009, 125). Traditional anti-Semitism "remained limited by many other kinds of social interactions among neighbors or colleagues" (Fritzsche 2009, 120). What made anti-Semitism strident among National Socialists was reducing, almost from one day to the other, "the different approaches toward neighbors . . . into the overriding distinction between Germans and Jews" (Fritzsche 2009, 120). This is what paved the way for the "social death," the "cold pogrom" that took place on an everyday basis (Fritzsche 2009, 125).

This is what a jailed Hutu, accused of participating in the murder of Tutsis between May and June 1994, said in Rilima Prison:

I was born surrounded by Tutsis in Kanazi. I always had Tutsi acquaintances and thought nothing of it. Still, I did grow up listening to history lessons and radio programs that were always talking about major problems between Hutus and Tutsis—though I lived among Tutsis that posed no problem. The situation was going to pieces due to the impossible gap between the worrisome news about the mess on the country's border and the peaceful people who lived next door. The situation was bound to come apart and to go into either savagery or neighborliness. (Hatzfeld 2005, 167–68)

Neighborliness or savagery: the alternatives are tremendously well presented. As we know, savagery won out.

Separated Although Close

I would like to draw attention to the ethical relevance of a feeling of neighborliness, the consciousness of belonging to one single space of coexistence. Ethical preoccupation never goes any further than the community of mutual acceptance from which it stems. The ethical gaze does not go beyond the boundary of the social world from which it emanates. We become moral people when we recognize ourselves as part of a framework of connections that bind us together with other people who we consider to be co-whatever: companions, contemporaries, colleagues, compatriots, and so on. The ethical preoccupation, the preoccupation for the consequences that our actions (and our omissions) have on other people, is a phenomenon that has something to do with accepting these other people as legitimate others with whom we can coexist. Only if we accept the other, is he or she visible to us. Is this paradoxical? No. All seeing involves looking. We only see what we look at. Something is only visible if we previously acknowledge it to be worthy of recognition. And being recognized implies not being strange, because strange implies anything that does not fit into our map of the world.

From this one might contend that the key critique in any reflection on solidarity must have something to do with achieving that community of mutual acceptance—that moral community from which the rights and responsibilities of solidarity make sense: "Am I my brother's keeper?" replies Cain when God asks him where Abel is. The story of Genesis tells us that when Cain said this, he had just killed his brother. Therefore his words might represent an attempt to cover up his crime—something along the lines of "I don't know what you are talking about," "it was not me," or "what are you talking about?"—as a means of avoiding his responsibility after the crime. In reality, Cain's evasive question is not the result of fratricide but its cause. It only occurs after the crime chronologically: Abel's murder was only possible because beforehand Cain had decided that he was not his brother's keeper, that there was no interdependent connection between them, and that Abel's destiny was not something he should feel responsible for. As noted, a human community is impossible without a moral community, without recognizing the other, without our mutual dependence and the responsibility derived thereof. Thus, a human community is only possible if we reply positively to Cain's question: "Yes, I am my brother's keeper." Further still, a human community is only possible if we do not ask this question—only if we do not need to ask this question because we consider it fully and legitimately answered (Bauman 2001, 72).

Nevertheless, one consequence of the moral individualism (and its flip side, moral fundamentalism) characteristic of our age is the miniaturization of the community. It is not so much a question of solidarity disappearing—on the contrary, it can even increase: references to "us" are increasingly important nowadays, and form the basis of the emergence of all kinds of localisms, ethnicisms, nationalisms, and fundamentalisms. Rather, solidarity is being more and more reduced to smaller and unconnected circles. Here, then, there is a first critical fissure in solidarity: it is compatible with exclusion, even in its most barbarous forms. The fiercest within-group solidarity aimed at preserving the group itself can coincide with and even encourage brutal confrontation with outside-group elements and their elimination. It is easy to respond to Cain's question by taking it literally: "Yes, you are your brother Abel's keeper." It is easy to note the twist contained in this question: "How can you ever doubt your responsibility toward your blood brother!" It is not so easy, however, to resolve another question: "To what point—to whom—does my responsibility extend?" To put this question another way: "Where are the limits of my responsibility toward others?"

In an excellent study on the origins and development of European racism and genocide, Sven Lindqvist argues that, to a large extent, colonialism (with all its great brutality) was possible thanks to the exercise of power without any form of control; this in practice made the colonizers invisible:

> The men representing civilization out in the colonies were "invisible" not only in the sense that their guns killed at a distance, but also in that no one at home really knew what they were doing. Cut off from their native country by enormous distances, poor communications and impenetrable jungles, they exercised imperial power without any control from home. (1996, 77)

How did they use power when there was no control? What transformation did they themselves go through when no one could longer watch over them? Through a discussion of the 1838 lectures of Herman Merivale at Oxford, Lindqvist proposes answers to these questions: "The main reason is that 'civilization' out there in the wilderness is represented by 'the trader, the backwoodsman, the pirate, the bushranger'; to put it briefly, by whites who can do anything they like with no risk of criticism or control" (1996, 123).

Yesterday there were insuperable distances, impenetrable forests, and bad communications; today there are no distances, forests are being reduced to a minimum, and communications have converted the planet into a global village. Yet the situation is the same: white people who can do whatever they want without running the risk of being attacked or controlled. This is because the brutality of nineteenth-century colonialism is explained not by geographical distance but by social distance.

"Exterminate," recalls Lindqvist, comes from the Latin *ex terminus*, meaning to push or drive over the border (*terminus*) (1996, 8). In Nazi Germany social distance fulfilled the same function as geographical distance in the Congo when it was converted into private property by King Leopold II of Belgium.

All of this does not just apply to Nazi Germany; nor is it merely a feature of the past. The weekly *Le Nouvel Observateur* (no. 2142, November 24–30, 2005) published an extensive report, "The New Aristocrats of Capitalism," coinciding with the apogee of riots in the urban peripheries of Paris in late 2005: "The suburbs are aflame, the CAC 40 [Paris stock market] is rising. . . . Everything has been said. Seldom was an economic elite so disconnected from the culture of its country. For these '*aristocacs*' [play on the word CAC] the only thing that counts is the world." While cars burned in the suburbs, the CAC 40 did not stop rising. In effect, everything has been said. Never before had an economic elite been so disconnected from the society in its own country. For these new "aristocrats" the only thing of importance was the world as a whole.

Zygmunt Bauman has dedicated many pages throughout his works to theorizing on the new features of power in times of globalization. He sees this as based less on the capacity to control (essentially spaces and people) and more on the capacity to emancipate oneself from any control, abrogating one's responsibility to manage spaces and society—a power that resides less in the capacity to oblige people to do things and more in not feeling obliged to do something dictated by others:

> In the present-day world mobility has become the most powerful and most coveted stratifying factor; the stuff from which the new, increasingly worldwide social, political, economic and cultural hierarchies are daily built and rebuilt. The mobility acquired by the owners and managers of capital means a new, indeed unprecedented in its radical unconditionality, disengagement of power from obligations: from duties towards employees, but also duties towards the younger and weaker, or yet unborn generations and towards self-reproduction of the living conditions of all; in short, freedom from the duty to contribute to daily life and the perpetuation of the community. There is a new asymmetry emerging between the extraterritorial nature of power and the continuing territoriality of the "whole life"—which the now unanchored powers, able to move at short notice or without warning, are free to exploit and abandon to the consequences of that exploitation. Shedding responsibility for consequences is the most coveted and cherished gain that the new mobility brings to free-floating, locally unbound capital. (Bauman 2001, 188–89)

What is the nature of this power that offers mobility? That of non-responsibility: "Whoever is free to run away from locality, is free to run away from the consequences" (Bauman 1998, 8–9). In this way, the contrast is evident between "the extraterritoriality of the new elite and the forced territoriality of the rest" (Bauman 1998, 23).

This new elite breaks all ties with its social environment, reduced to a mere biographical accident or simple historical moment: "The people of the 'upper tier' do not apparently belong to the place they inhabit. Their concerns lie (or rather float) elsewhere . . . they have no vested interests in the city in which their residences are located. . . . They are therefore, by and large, *unconcerned* with the affairs of 'their' city—just one locality among many, all of them small and insignificant from the vantage point of cyberspace, their genuine, even if virtual, home" (Bauman 2003, 16). Their maximum aspiration is to have "a wider scope of their mobility" (Bauman 2003, 20) and thus, if things get bad, they always have the option of moving on.

The new global class, far from the perverse consequences that provoke its apparently rational decisions, seems to have increasingly opted for a strategy of resident expatriatism (Kaplan 2000, 92–93). Even when it is "here," its idea of here is very different from the societies that surround it. This class takes refuge in its gated communities, true voluntary ghettos (Bauman 2003, 29), self-chosen prisons that close themselves off from the exterior with the aim of isolating anyone outside; in these exclusive spaces they "opt out of the public sphere and the 'social contract'" in return for a protected environment (Kaplan 2000, 84). This is the secession of the successful (Reich 1991) by those for whom "communities have become commodities" (Reich 2002, 98), by those whose connection to local spaces is based on strictly individual and essentially economic interests, in such a way that in their relations with these communities they rigorously apply the principle of rational choice: obtain maximum benefit from minimum cost.

Referring to this situation, Amitai Etzioni condemns the fact that neoliberal reform since the 1990s has resulted in a "widespread sense of deprivation, insecurity, anxiety, pessimism, and anger" (1996, 81). He concludes by questioning to what extent society can go on tolerating public and business policies that continue to give free rein to financial interests without, in doing so, undermining the moral legitimacy of the social order. We do not know how much, but we do know what happens when these policies become dominant: "To the deliberate atrophy of the welfare state corresponds the dystopic hypertrophy of the penal state," contends Loïc Wacquant (2009, 58).

The Call for Neighborliness

Faced with the major possibility of the social bond breaking down—major, although without arriving at the extreme of the Nazi Holocaust, the Rwandan genocide, or the ethnic cleansing in the former Yugoslavia—there is only one responsible option: to develop practices of managing diversity that allow, as the titles of several works by Leonie Sandercock (2000) call for, strangers to become neighbors, as a means of combating the dangerous opposite tendency: making certain neighbors strangers. And in order to do so, it is not sufficient to just *live together yet apart*, to use Juan Carlos Checa's (2007) accurate expression in his study of the spatial segregation of African immigrants in Almería, Andalusia.

As noted earlier, one need not just think of the terrible breakdowns of human coexistence witnessed in the twentieth century or "the century of genocides" (Bruneteau 2004) to underscore how important it is to affirm neighborliness as opposed to the segregationist dynamics of othering—of casting others as foreigners or strangers. This is because, while the potential outcomes of courses of action that lead othering to violence are certainly quite different, what concerns me with such a reflection is warning about the very link between othering and these potential courses of action and itself. "Political and intellectual discourse," warns José María Ridao,

> should be wary of detecting when that succession of fatal errors begins that affects the bases of coexistence, and which gradually deprives us of the options in which humanism and piety are still possible, in which the life of one single individual is still more important than all doctrines, in order to leave us at the end of the journey faced with dilemmas in which suffering and devastation no longer matter. (2002, 162–63)

I share this warning fully.

In the summer of 2009 there were significant problems in a town in Gipuzkoa related to a supposed rise in criminal acts, with the arrest of a Maghrebi minor accused of sexual assault the ultimate detonator, and which resulted in a conflict with xenophobic connotations. The municipal authorities reacted swiftly by getting involved in the issue and with apparently good results, given that the incidents stopped in a matter of days. Nevertheless, a declaration by the authorities stands out, made undoubtedly with the best of intentions but which leads one to think that what happened in that town was more a question of temporary calm than a long-term solution: "Next week, alongside specialist experts in conflict-resolution, we are going to try and resolve the problem by bringing together locals and Maghrebis. The idea is to act as mediators" (*El Correo*, July 11, 2009). Is it not the case that those Maghrebis who live there and whose work and businesses are there are also locals? The declarations of another local leader are infinitely more worrying. According to Xavier García Albiol, head of the PP's municipal group in the city hall of Badalona, Catalonia, "If I am elected mayor next year and the downturn that is about to take place comes about, between giving social welfare to an illegal immigrant or to a local of Badalona, I am very clear on the matter" (*Público*, January 22, 2010). Locals *against* Maghrebis, immigrants *against* locals, without any exaggeration—these are extremely worrying approaches.

The Albanian writer Ismail Kadare begins his work *Three Elegies for Kosovo* thus:

> There were times when the peninsula seemed truly large, with enough space for everyone: for different languages and faiths, for a dozen peoples, states, kingdoms and principalities—even for three empires, two of which, the Serbian and the Bulgarian, were now in ruins, with the result that the third, the Byzantine Empire, was to its disgrace, and that of all Christianity, declared a Turkish vassal.
>
> But times changed, and with them the ideas of the local people changed, and the peninsula began to seem quite constricting. This feeling of constriction was spawned more from the ancient memories of the people than by their lands and languages rubbing against each other. In their solitude the people hatched nightmares until one day they felt they could no longer bear it. (2000, 3–4)

It is a mistake to think that savagery happens to us; in reality, "savagery is chosen" (Ridao 2002, 167). For that reason, there is no better way to prevent collective violence, or to try to, than combating those nightmares that peoples tend to think about in solitude, with bovine stubbornness, feeding on grievance and fear, until they feel that there is no room for everyone; which is a way of saying that there is no longer room for "them": the others.

References

Améry, Jean. 1980. *At the Mind's Limits: Contemplations by a Survivor on Auschwitz and Its Reality*. Translated by Sidney Rosenfeld and Stella P. Rosenfeld. Bloomington: Indiana University Press.

Andrić, Ivo. 1959. *The Bridge on the Drina*. Translated by Lovett F. Edwards. London: Allen & Unwin.

Appadurai, Arjun. 2006. *Fear of Small Numbers: An Essay on the Geography of Anger*. Durham, NC: Duke University Press.

Attali, Jacques. 1991. *Millennium: Winners and Losers in the Coming World Order*. Translated by Leila Conners and Nathan Gardels. New York: Times Books.

Bauman, Zygmunt. 1997. *Postmodernity and Its Discontents*. New York: New York University Press.

———. 1998. *Globalization: The Human Consequences*. New York: Columbia University Press.

———. 2000. *Modernity and the Holocaust*. New York: Cornell University Press.

———. 2001. *The Individualized Society*. Cambridge: Polity Press.

———. 2003. *City of Fears, City of Hopes*. London: Goldsmiths College, University of London.

Bauman, Zygmunt, and Keith Tester. 2001. *Conversations with Zygmunt Bauman*. Malden, MA: Blackwell.

Beck, Ulrich. 1996. "How Neighbors Become Jews: The Political Construction of the Stranger in an Age of Reflexive Modernity." *Constellations* 2, no. 3: 378–96.

———. 1998. *Democracy without Enemies*. Translated by Mark Ritter. Malden, MA: Polity Press.

———. 2004. "Cosmopolitical Realism: On the Distinction between Cosmopolitanism in Philosophy and the Social Sciences." *Global Networks* 4, no. 2: 131–56.

Berger, Peter L., and Thomas Luckmann. 1995. *Modernity, Pluralism and the Crisis of Meaning: The Orientation of Modern Man*. Gütersloh, Germany: Bertelsmann Foundation Publishers.

Bruneteau, Bernard. 2004. *Le siècle des génocides: Violences, massacres et processus génocidaires de l'Arménie au Rwanda*. Paris: A. Colin.

Checa, Juan Carlos. 2007. *Viviendo juntos aparte: La segregación espacial de los africanos en Almería*. Barcelona: Icaria.

Droit, Roger-Pol. 2009. *Genealogía de los bárbaros*. Translated by Núria Petit Fontseré. Barcelona: Paidós. French version: *Généalogie des barbares*. Paris: Jacob, 2007.

Etzioni, Amitai. 1996. *The New Golden Rule: Community and Morality in a Democratic Society*. New York: Basic Books.

Finkielkraut, Alain. 2001. *La ingratitud: Conversación sobre nuestro tiempo*. Translated by Francisco Díez del Corral. Barcelona: Anagrama. French version: *L'ingratitude: Conversation sur notre temps avec Antoine Robitaille*. Montreal: Éditions Québec Amérique, 1999.

Fritzsche, Peter. 2009. *Life and Death in the Third Reich*. Cambridge, MA: Belknap Press.

Gellately, Robert. 2001. *Backing Hitler: Consent and Coercion in Nazi Germany*. Oxford: Oxford University Press.

Gross, Jan T. 2001. *Neighbors: The Destruction of the Jewish Community in Jedwabne, Poland*. Princeton, NJ: Princeton University Press.

Hatzfeld, Jean. 2005. *Machete Season: The Killers in Rwanda Speak, A Report*. Translated by Linda Coverdale. Preface by Susan Sontag. New York: Farrar, Straus and Giroux.

Kadare, Ismail. 2000. *Three Elegies for Kosovo*. Translated by Peter Constantine. London: Harvill Press.

Kaplan, Robert D. 2000. *The Coming Anarchy: Shattering the Dreams of the Cold War*. New York: Random House.

Kertész, Imre. 2002. *Yo, otro: Crónica del cambio*. Translated by Adan Kovacsics. Barcelona: El Acantilado. Hungarian version: *Valaki más: A változás krónikája*. Budapest: Magvető.

Klemperer, Victor. 2006. *The Language of the Third Reich: LTI-Lingua Tertii Imperii, A Philologist's Notebook*. Translated by Martin Brady. London: Continuum.

Lévy, Bernard-Henri. 1996. *La pureza peligrosa*. Translated by Berta Corral and Mercedes Corral. Madrid: Espasa. French version: *La pureté dangereuse*. Paris: B. Grasset, 1994.

Lindqvist, Sven. 1996. *Exterminate All the Brutes: One Man's Odyssey into the Heart of Darkness and the Origins of European Genocide*. Translated by Joan Tate. New York: Free Press.

Mazower, Mark. 1999. *Dark Continent: Europe's Twentieth Century*. New York: Alfred A. Knopf.

Nancy, Jean Luc. 1996. "La existencia exiliada." *Archipiélago* 26–27: 34–40.

Reich, Robert B. 1991. "Secession of the Successful." *New York Times Magazine*, January 20. www-personal.umich.edu/~gmarkus/secession.html.

———. 2002. *The Future of Success: Working and Living in the New Economy*. New York: Vintage Books.

Ridao, José María. 2002. *La elección de la barbarie: Liberalismo frente a ciudadanía en la sociedad*. Barcelona: Tusquets.

Sandercock, Leonie. 2000. "When Strangers Become Neighbours: Managing Cities of Difference." *Planning Theory & Practice* 1: 13–30.

Sanmartín, José. February 2008. "Preocuparse por parchear el ejercicio de la violencia, cuando esta ya ha surgido, sirve sólo para sacar rédito político." *Teína* 17. www.revistateina.org/teina17/dos6.htm.

Simmel, Georg. 1950. "The Stranger." In *The Sociology of Georg Simmel*, translated, edited, and with an introduction by Kurt H. Wolff. New York: Free Press.

Sofsky, Wolfgang. 2003. *Violence: Terror, Genocide, War*. Translated by Anthea Bell. London: Granta.

Stouffer, Samuel A. 1949. *The American Soldier*. Princeton, NJ: Princeton University Press.

Thorup, Mikkel. 2006. "Cosmopolitics!" *Le Monde Diplomatique* 4. www.eurozine.com/articles/2006-04-10-thorup-en.html.

Todorov, Tzvetan. 2003. *Hope and Memory: Lessons from the Twentieth Century*. Translated by David Bellos. Princeton, NJ: Princeton University Press.

Wacquant, Loïc. 2009. *Prisons of Poverty*. Minneapolis: University of Minnesota Press.

Zubero, Imanol. 2010. *Confianza ciudadana y capital social en sociedades multiculturales*. Bilbao: Ikuspegi.

3

In the Limbo of the Invisible

CARMEN AROCENA and NEKANE E. ZUBIAUR

Translated by Cameron J. Watson

> When the infinite servitude of the woman disappears, when she lives for and by herself, and the man, until now abominable, has returned what belongs to her, she will also be a poet. Will their world of ideas be different to ours? They will find out strange, unfathomable, repulsive, delicious things; we will embrace them, understand them.
>
> — Arthur Rimbaud

The lives of all human beings can be understood as a narration in which each one joins together with and breaks away from different objects of desire. In *Semiotics and Language* the French semiotician Algirdas Julien Greimas and coauthor Joseph Courtés define narrative schema as "a kind of formal framework within which is recorded 'life meaning' with its three essential domains: the qualification of the subject, which introduces it into life; its 'realization,' by means of which it 'acts'; and finally the sanction—at one and the same time retribution and recognition—which alone guarantees the meaning of its actions and installs it as a subject of being" (1982, 204). Therefore, we desire and act, and are evaluated by it.

The long history of feminist demands could be understood as the union of women, considered as generic subjects, who share different objects of value in contrast to those they have been traditionally disconnected from (the vote, access to the labor market, and so on). Evidently, this struggle of women toward their union with freedom—in other words, the capacity to come together with any object of value allowed to men in contemporary society—is not as paramount as it appears. Rather, the female gender has been subjected to a process of manipulation—also prevalent in all narrations—that in this case takes the form of a tangible agent, traditionally termed *patriarchal society*, which has defined what women could do, must do, know how to do, and, as a consequence, want to do. Greimas and Courtés define manipulation as "an action of humans upon other humans with the goal of having them carry out a given program," or, in sum, "causing-to-do." This is a communication in which "the destinator-manipulator pushes the receiver-manipulatee toward a position wherein freedom is lacking (not-being-able-not-to-do), to the point that the latter is obliged to accept the proposed contract." This "not-being-able-not-to-do" would be the equivalent of defining the obedience of the manipulated in the face of the manipulator (Greimas and Courtés 1982, 184).

The struggles for equality have gone a step toward independence, defined by Greimas and Courtés as a position marked by a "being-able-to-not-doing." Yet current patriarchal society, which in appearance has assimilated female emancipation, disguises this situation of independence deceitfully under the umbrella of that absolute liberty ("being-able-to-do-doing") that becomes the long-desired-for goal. In this chapter we attempt to demonstrate the false nature of this freedom and how patriarchy denies the power to enter into conjunction with some objects of desire, using the symbolic imaginary constructed and diffused in audiovisual representations by the mass communications media, which is in itself a tacit form of violence that does not just, or alone, operate physically against women.

The *Merriam-Webster Unabridged Dictionary* defines "violence," among other things, as "injury in the form of revoking, repudiation, distortion, infringement, or irreverence to a thing, notion, or quality fitly valued or observed," and the word "violent," among other things, as "furious or vehement to the point of being improper, unjust, or illegal." The first of these definitions implies that submission to the obedience of the patriarchy means the negation of attributes integral to women's nature. The second refers to a future phase of sanction in which inadequate compartments will be judged by a court that is no other but patriarchal society itself, which dictates what is correct and incorrect, appropriate and inappropriate. Greimas and Courtés's semiotic theory breaks apart this process in the following way:

Manipulation plays upon persuasion and thus articulates the persuasive doing of the sender and the interpretative doing of the receiver.

(a) The manipulator can exercise its persuasive doing by relying on the modality of being-able: on the pragmatic side it will propose either positive objects (cultural values) or negative objects (threats) to the one manipulated. In other instances the manipulator will persuade the receiver with the help of knowing: on the cognitive side it will bring the receiver to know what the manipulator thinks of the former's modal competence Thus is appears that persuasion in terms of being-able characterizes temptation (where a positive object of value is proposed) and intimidation (presentation of a negative gift); persuasion in terms of knowing is peculiar to provocation (with a negative judgment: "You are incapable of . . ." and seduction (manifesting a positive judgment). (1982, 184–85)

In both cases, the ultimate goal pursued by the destinator-manipulator is that of accepting as true the message transmitted by means of intervention (doing-believing) and impediment (doing-not-believing) in order to make the receiver carry out a specific narrative program (action) to the detriment of others. Patriarchal society exercises its persuasive "doing" on women in the form of both "being-able-to-do" and "knowing-how-to-do," and it uses the media as delegated actors in order to carry out the four forms of manipulation mentioned. Consequently, in the terrain of media images there is an attempt to achieve doing-believing by means of doing-seeing, and doing-not-believing by doing-not seeing.

This is not the moment to go more into the well-known issue about the influence that the media exert on social behavior through iconizing mechanisms. It is instead interesting to analyze how certain female representations and certain activities that sociological and psychological studies consider common disappear from media messages, and, as a consequence, other behaviors are exalted and transformed into a standard of unreal, and hence unachievable, conduct. All these are related to women's sexual desire.

The Object of Ideal Desire: Beauty

The history of humanity has been characterized by the imposition of a common desire on the female part of society: that of joining in with what each epoch called "beauty" as a means of dominating the overwhelming power over nature that resided in women and terrified men. Works of art reflect in figurative form what is considered beautiful at the moment they are created, thereby endowing this with meaning to the world; from what one might deduce from the notion that "the role of art in society is not simply to provide the consumer with sensitive gratification. Art is a guide, a means of instruction, and I would say almost of learning about the ambient reality" (Merquior 1978, 51). By extension, the images on offer by the media also fulfill an identical function. Camille Paglia, in her consideration of the origins of beauty, argues that "there is . . . nothing beautiful in nature. Nature is primal power, coarse and turbulent. Beauty is our weapon against nature; by it we make objects, giving them limit, symmetry, proportion. Beauty halts and freezes the melting flux of nature" (1990, 57). Clearly, Paglia identifies women with the creative force of nature. In her opinion, "male bonding and patriarchy were the recourse to which man was forced by his terrible sense of woman's power, her imperviousness, he archetypal confederacy with chthonian nature" (1990, 12). However, although it is Dionysius who governs chthonic forces, Paglia observes that Western civilization—and consequently *its eye*—are to a great extent Apollonian and dominated by reason and logic:

> I believe that the aesthetic sense, like everything else thus far, is a swerve from the chthonian. . . . The eye is peremptory in its judgments. It decides what to see and why. Each of our glances is as much exclusion as inclusion. . . . We see too much, and so have to stringently limit our seeing. Desire is besieged on all sides by anxiety and doubt. Beauty, an ecstasy of the eye, drugs us and allows us to act. Beauty is our Apollonian revision of the chthonian. (1990, 15–16)

Beauty, therefore, provides women with neither control nor freedom but is instead imposed on them as a grid of meaning that demonstrates what in a given era is worthy of being shown. We have thus been influenced by the fact that in the contemporary system of the visible there are only young, beautiful, anatomically perfect, slim, and symmetrical bodies. Showing bodily aging or skin or anatomical deformity flees the rules and forms part of that space that cannot be iconized; because this cannot be molded into a signifier, it never forms part of the imaginary that reflects reality. As Polly Young-Eisendrath remarks:

> There is no way to remain completely free from this message that female power is beauty. As girls and women we live and breathe this atmosphere. It pervades all we do and all the ways we are reflected back to ourselves. In the media there is rarely a female accomplishment that is unaccom-

panied by a description of what the woman was wearing and/or how she looked. It is as if we must survey a woman's appearance either to find the root of her success in beauty (so she can be reduced to her appearance) or in its absence to explain her success in terms of compensating for her lack of that essential ingredient. For a majority of American [and other] women appearance becomes the central expression of personal identity. (1999, 35)

Female identity always oscillates between the virtues of being and the tyranny of appearing,[1] imposed by the images that bombard us from the media and that exert a violence as harmful as that which is invoked under the name of domestic violence; insofar as it directly affects the way in which we construct our symbolic imaginary and, therefore, our form of experiencing reality, resulting in the fact that anything that cannot be expressed or shown becomes inexistent. Patriarchal society obliges women to accept the defining rules or cultural canons of beauty in forcing them to believe that their connection to the object of value ("beauty") will be rewarded positively with happiness, success, or personal satisfaction, by means of that method Greimas and Courtés define as *temptation*, a positive gift that the manipulator offers the manipulatee.

Structural semiotics has adapted to iconic language Louis Hjelmslev's famous division between the expression plane and the content plane:

> *Content material* is common to all semiotic phenomena although content material only exists that is identified with what we call meaning (the semantic fabric, the entire universe of meaning). What varies from one system of meaning to another is the separation of this semantic fabric into relevant units: *content form*, or rather the system itself of meanings, the organization into a system of operations, and differences in the content material (Zunzunegui 1985, 108–9).

As a consequence, women are material without a sufficient form.

The fact that the patriarchy exhibits beauty and youth as a positive value relegates ugliness and old age to the realm of the invisible, locating this object of value under the threat of not forming part of society; of not being important; of lacking basic human attributes like the capacity to love, to feel, or, ultimately, to live. This manipulative activity that consists of doing-not-seeing uses, therefore, forms of *intimidation* to prevail.

---

1. It is no coincidence that in the section on "veridiction," Algirdas Julien Greimas and Joseph Courtés (1982, 369) consider "seeming" and "being" to be two opposing terms.

Some artists have applied the form grid to content material in order to visualize bodies considered deformed according to the canon of traditional beauty (the dwarves, giants, and freaks that parade before the lens of Diane Arbus, for example), with the aim of integrating them into the terrain of normality, demanding tolerance, compassion, and equality. Thus, "in a society in which the warped are supposedly normal, having to look for some forms of the strange means on the side of the standard. In the same way that giants and dwarves, trapped by their objective in ordinary moments of existence, become human, likewise a parade of 'normal' bodies, surprised in the public space, exudes strangeness" (Courtine 2006, 256).

This is the case of a work by Les Krims titled *My Mother Extruding Her False Teeth as Her Mother Did to Scare Children* (1970). In the image we see the photographer's elderly mother sitting nude next to a window while she takes out her dentures. Converting a normal (although nude) aged body undertaking an everyday act into material that can be displayed is inevitably perverted by the observer's gaze, which only sees a grotesque monstrosity in the morbid layers of skin brought on by old age.

These values that surround beauty are ingrained in us from childhood, when our ideas are still virgin terrain on which all kinds of dictates are sown that will indelibly mark us well into adulthood. Fairy tales are the most efficient tool to do this. Every time an ugly or monstrous character appears in children's stories that we are encouraged to accept socially because of their good virtues, it always ends up with the promise of their transformation into another state that is aesthetically acceptable. This is the case of *Beauty and the Beast* and *The Ugly Duckling*, a story line adopted recently in the Colombian soap opera *Yo soy Betty, la fea* (1999), which was remade for US television as *Ugly Betty* (2006). Only the subversive animation series *Shrek* (directed by Andrew Adamson and Vicky Jensen for the first time in 2001) has dared to transgress these principles and invert the politically correct imaginary created by the Disney factory, in its suggestion of ugliness as a value that is far from contemptible. In these Dreamworks productions it is not the frog that is transformed into a prince, but rather the princess who is transformed into an ogre in order to lead a more satisfying life.

However, the transgressive ogre still enjoys the privilege of being young. Female aging has been defined by Susan Sontag (1972, in Kauffman 1998, 87) as "a process of becoming obscene. . . . That old women are repulsive is one of the most profound esthetic and erotic feelings in our culture," faced with which the female spectator discovers the gratifying sensation of still "not being me." In the history of film elderly women have always been presented dressed and asexual, except in a recent exception that implies one of the few transgressions offered us by cinematography in this regard.

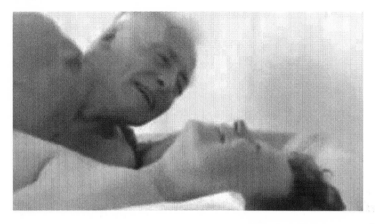

This is a German film titled *Cloud 9* (*Wolke 9*, Andreas Dresen, 2008), which tells the love story between Inge (Ursula Wener) and Karl (Horst Westphal), both septuagenarians. Their relationship begins like a sexual explosion, which shocks Inge's feelings for her husband, Werner (Horst Rehberg), to whom she has been married for over thirty years. Despite being unable to return to her routine daily existence, her relationship with Karl leads to profound feelings of guilt for the woman, who ends up confessing her adultery to her husband. Inge receives neither understanding nor absolution from him, and as a result the marriage breaks down and she goes off with her lover in search of happiness. Dressen's camera portrays the elderly bodies in playful sex scenes, emphasized by strong lighting and colorless sets to express the happiness and abundance of the two lovers. They are not punished, but instead enjoy a bright and happy ending in contrast to the darkness into which her marriage had unfolded, and in which sexual relations among senior citizens have always existed in the sociocultural imaginary.

The Sexual Form of Phallocentrism

Sexual relations among the elderly are not the only invisible element in the mass media in contemporary society. Shere Hite revolutionized sociological theory in the mid-1970s with the publication of the *Hite Report*, whose aim was to "demonstrate and define sex as an institution that reflects the different status between men and women within society, which had never taken the female body into consideration" (Bouchard and Froissart 2004, 12). Hite (1981) saw the sexual organ, the source of female pleasure, as absent not just in representations of coitus in art, photography, and film, but also in the specialist literature, when she discovered that 70 percent of women polled in order to draw up her report only obtained pleasure by mans of clitoral stimulation, and not by penetration. This issue has remained mute for a long time, although some manuals that are still designed to help orient women sexually today, such as that of Sylvia de Béjar (2009), thirty years after Hite, recall it periodically. Nevertheless, certain details lead us to believe that this silent process reflects the needs of a specific cultural era that goes back to the dawn of time. The figure of Lilith,[2] Adam's first wife, has been eliminated by the Christian tradition because of her independence and her desire to feel equal to men, even in sexual relations, given that the couple formed by the first man and the first (and forgotten) woman "never found peace, mainly because Lilith, not wishing to renounce her equality, argued with her companion about the way and form of undertaking carnal union" (Bornay 1995, 25), or, what amounts to the same thing, seeking her own pleasure. Mythology converted her into a demonic being that attacked women in labor and devoured the children born of her innumerable lovers. She was, then, initially identified as a female figure who refuted maternity, to be later condemned to silence in favor of more maternal icons like Eve, the primitive ancestor of all men, and Mary, the archetypal mother par excellence.

If mythology recognizes the existence of the first woman who sought her own pleasure, then specialists as early as the sixteenth century also studied the source of this pleasure in scholarly ways, as Naomi Wolf (1997) reminds us:

> A Venetian scientist, Renaldus Columbus, called the clitoris "the seat of woman's delight" and provided a detailed description of orgasm through manipulation of it. Because of women's possibilities of sustained sexual pleasure, they were often described as the more sexually driven of the two sexes. Physicians and midwives recommended sensitive and thorough stimulation of the clitoris on all occasions of lovemaking, especially as incentive and preparation for conception, as a way to satisfy female

---

2. The first references to the myth of Lilith appear in a Midrash, a text interpreting the Jewish Torah, in the twelfth century.

sexual desire so that women would not become agitated and restless in a state of unsatisfied desire. (Quoted in Young-Eisendrath 1999, 61)

If women were so sexually insatiable, how could one man hope to possess and control them?

Freud converted the phallus (its presence, absence, and desire) into the yardstick of human sexuality, forcing women into an incessant search for all they had been deprived of. This issue has caused much discussion and still unresolved debates at the heart of psychology, although the opinion expressed by Claude Alzon (1982, 17) would seem more a matter of basic common sense:

> In a system that essentially sees sexual behavior as derived, it is essential to know what this consist of from the beginning. One should believe a priori that men and women, as a consequence of having different sexualities, would experience different behaviors. Nonetheless, this common sense solution is not that defended by Freud. Appearing most strange in that lifelong dubious belief, from a very early moment Freud stuck to the seemingly fatuous idea, and never wavered despite all the criticism, that only one sexuality existed. . . . From men and women having two qualitatively different libidos, Freud made them naturally equal, relegating male power to the relativity of culture. But in giving them the same sexuality, that of the male, he established a qualitative difference that would condemn women forever, condemned by nature to obey.

Men thus became the measure of desire, whether male or female and despite their biological differences, which forced women to deny their own sexuality in favor of that of men. Women converted images of a visualized sexuality into a desirable form of their way of experiencing carnal relations, even though this form had little to do with their own reality. Catharine A. MacKinnon (1982, 530–31) argues that,

> socially, femaleness means femininity, which means attractiveness to men, which means sexual attractiveness, which means sexual availability on male terms. What defines women as such is what turns men on. Good girls are "attractive," bad girls "provocative." Gender socialization is the process through which women come to identify themselves as sexual beings, as beings that exist for men. It is that process through which women internalize (make their own) a male image of their sexuality as their identity as women. It is not just an illusion.

Film, meanwhile, has converted penetration into the typical means of fulfilling sexual passion between protagonists, banishing any specifically female representation of clitoral pleasure in favor of phallocentric coital penetration and burying in the terrain of the elliptical all the preliminaries necessary to favor female ardor, which in images always occurs simultaneously alongside male arousal.

For this reason, Teresa de Lauretis (1984, 67) points out that "it is men who have defined the 'visible things' of cinema, who have defined the object and modality of vision, pleasure, and meaning on the basis of perceptional and conceptual schemata provided by patriarchal ideological and social formations. In the frame of reference of men's cinema, narrative, and visual theories, the male is the measure of desire." The perfection of sexual chemistry from a male point of view is exemplified in the torrid copulation on a kitchen table between Jack Nicholson and Jessica Lange in *The Postman Always Rings Twice* (Bob Rafelson, 1981), the use of butter as a lubricant in *Last Tango in Paris* (Bernardo Bertolucci, 1972), and the numerous sex scenes that made Kim Basinger and Mickey Rourke famous in *9 1/2 Weeks* (Adrian Lyne, 1986). The media owned by patriarchal society publicize these kinds of phallocentric sexual encounters repeatedly, using a manipulative method over women termed *seduction*, which informs the female world what a perfect sexual relationship is, to which they should aspire for their own enjoyment.

Yet in film everything is a lie and on very few occasions do filmmakers dare to reflect penetration as an experience devoid of any attraction from the female point of view. Hite's studies confirm that

> there is still an enormous distance between what women say they feel in a sexual relationship, how they have an orgasm, and what the public image represents in this regard. Hollywood films, sex videos, and internet pornography continue to show women who imitate men sexually and act like male fantasies about women: they try and have an orgasm by means of the same stimulation as men (coitus). (Hite 2002, 42)

In this regard, one can highlight two extremely significant examples that each demonstrate different but quite normal reactions in a patriarchal sexual relationship that disregards the existence of the female sexual organ: pain and dissatisfaction.

In *Kadosh* (1999), the Israeli filmmaker Amos Gitai narrates the parallel lives of two couples in an ultra-Orthodox environment in Jerusalem. The first of these is made up by Meir and Rivka, who, although they love

each other, are forced to break up because the community rabbi assumes that Meir is incapable of conceiving children. Rivka must choose a new wife with whom he can procreate, thereby demonstrating Meir's sterility. Meanwhile, Meir's sister, Malka, will be forced to marry a religious fundamentalist, Yossef, despite being in love with a young man who leads a modern lifestyle. Gitai dissects Yossef and Malka's first sexual encounter with his camera. After shaving off all her hair (a symbol of female beauty, now of no use in her new state), Malka lies in bed while Yossef prays before beginning a sexual encounter full of ineptitude and violence. There are no naked bodies in the scene, or caresses, or even kisses. Yossef lifts up his new wife's nightdress—who in the symbolic act of shaving her hair off has renounced her desires—and penetrates her clumsily and brutally while he hides her cries of pain by covering her mouth. Gitai filmed the scene in one single shot without the camera intervening or embellishing at any moment the coldness and cruelty of the act on show, thereby generating a profound sense of discomfort among anyone watching, who can only feel compassion for Malka. Gitai's choice to shoot the scene from a distance, closer to documentary-style filming, makes it a condemnation of sex without pleasure to honor God. Indeed, this is the main argument on which *Kadosh* is based: a film critical of Orthodox Judaism that highlights the complete absence of women's freedom in all aspects of their lives, including the realm of sexual pleasure as well.

Blissfully Yours (*Sud Sanaeha,* Apichatpong Weerasethakul, 2002) is an example of contemplative cinema in which the three protagonists (a young couple, Min and Roong, together with by Orn, a middle-aged female nurse) express their sexual instincts in a Thai jungle. Orn is in a

relationship with a forest ranger. Weerasethakul films the sexual act in a similar way to that of Gitai: in a fixed shot without the camera intervening in any way. On this occasion, however, the director's intrepid gaze has nothing to do with condemnation, but rather it remains in pure contemplation of a completely realist coitus far from the fantasy re-creations of commercial American cinema. And what the Thai filmmaker reflects is Orn's indifference throughout the scene shot in real time.

When the act is over, Orn (like Eve) offers her Adam an apple, perhaps in order to offer him that knowledge about female nature he lacks. Unsatisfied, Orn caresses her companion's navel as an unintelligible signal that relations have not yet finished for her; she later caresses her own before moving her fingers down into her panties and ends up guiding her companion's hand toward her clitoris. Weerasethakul shoots the scene

modestly in a brief shot that only shows the lovers' faces, leaving their sexual maneuvers out of shot, with the aim of focusing on the female face that, for the first time, reflects the beginning of pleasure. This pleasure is, however, cut short by the male's actions because he is more interested in eating the apple than satisfying his companion, and in a second attempt, by his escape toward an accidental death. For Orn, sexual satisfaction is impossible, as demonstrated by her tears toward the end of the film.

The Piano (Jane Campion, 1993) is one of the films that best represent symbolically the repressive violence that patriarchal society inflicts on women's sexual pleasure. Set in the nineteenth century, *The Piano* tells the story of Ada (Holly Hunter), forced to abandon her paternal home together with her daughter and move to the wilds of New Zealand in order to marry Stewart (Sam Neill), a potentate she barely knows. Subjected to the conventions of an oppressive society since she was a child, Ada chose to stop speaking at the age of six of her own free will, and she only communicates through the music of her piano that fires her passion. Stewart forbids his new wife from playing the piano (he abandons it on a beach so that he does not have to move the heavy object to his house), and she, in return, refuses to have sexual relations with him. Initially, the man accepts the woman's reticence as a sign of passing shyness and mistrust stemming from her new situation, but when he discovers that his wife has been unfaithful to him with a Maori called Baines (Harvey Keitel), it arouses his anger.

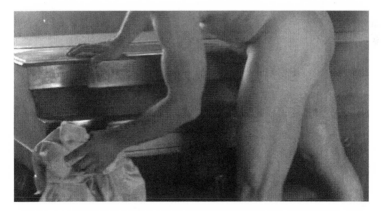

The sexual relationship between Baines and Ada is channeled through the piano. The instrument is the only form of expression the woman has to exteriorize her desires and feelings. Baines takes the piano to his house and promises to return it to her if she passes some tests of a clearly sexual nature while she plays for him. Each of these tests implies progress toward Ada's sexual liberation. The first day, she must allow Baines to caress a small hole in her stockings, the only and minute surface of naked skin that remains uncovered on her body; later, the Maori orders her to take off her black corseted dress until she is in her underwear; and when, ultimately, Ada gives her body physically to the man, she releases the braids tying up her hair in a gesture that is the opposite of Malka's in *Kadosh*.

The erotic encounters between Ada and Baines reach a metaphorical pinnacle before their full carnal union, in a sequence in which a completely naked Baines moves around the piano caressing it tenderly. The piano is Ada's body, the volcano of emotions and desires from which she takes out music that expresses her most intimate pleasure. In order to do this, Campion shows us Ada sliding her fingers sensually over the keys (erogenous spots) of her piano-body, in such a way that it is no coincidence that when Stewart, furious at Ada's rejection and infidelity, tries to show his power over her, he chooses to chop off her index finger, the source of her sexual pleasure, likening it, even physically, to the clitoris. We witness, then, a fully fledged symbolic ablation.

This ablation, presented symbolically in the film, almost forms part of the real action in that it proscribes to invisibility any kind of clitoral sexual relationship. And we already know that if something is not named, it does not exist, despite the fact that Hite (2002, 43) has spent a long time reminding us that "it is normal for women to have orgasms thanks to clitoral stimulation; it is neither immature nor dysfunctional. The way women reach orgasm is something to be celebrated, not criticized. It is not women who have sexual problems, but society that has problems in accepting and understanding women's sexuality."

The Nearsightedness of Pseudo-Feminist Glasses

In 2007, the Image Observatory of Spain's Women's Institute requested the Italian fashion company Dolce & Gabbana to remove an advertisement it considered to be humiliating toward women. In the press release issued by this body, it was stated that, from the advertisement "one might deduce that it is admissible to use force as a means of forcing oneself on women," adding that such images "imply a reinforcement of attitudes that are today illegal; they attack the rights of women and denigrate their image and in no way favor the work undertaken for many years in order to achieve equality with men."

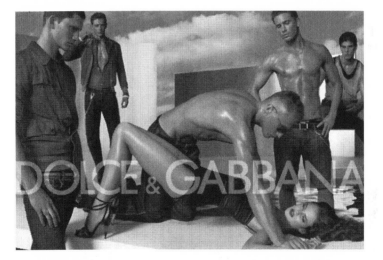

The history of Rome has retrieved Messalina, the wife of Emperor Claudius and known for her legendary lust, from anonymity. Messalina the nymphomaniac, according to the poet Juvenal's narration, drove her to challenging prostitutes in Rome, in an unusual competition, to see how many men they could sleep with in one day. The representative of the guild of ladies of the night, Escila, managed to have sexual relations with twenty-five. And the legend says that Messalina was only satisfied after lying with two hundred men. This is not a unique case. Erika Bornay (1995, 21) mentions Astarte, also known as Ishtar:

She is one of the most significant goddesses in Assyrian-Babylonian mythology and from which the Greek Aphrodite took many of her features. The cruel goddess of fertility, but also of war, love, and pleasure, she was irritable and violent and, in her capacity as sister of the queen of the underworld, she helped populate those places. Sacred prostitution was an integral part of the cult of Astarte, who had countless lovers that she only used to keep for an hour, sufficient time however to debase men with her woeful love.

It is not too much to state that Dolce & Gabbana was updating the myth of Messalina, a woman who chose men in order to enjoy pleasure. One might question the interpretation of the image as attempted group rape if one looks at the details missed completely by the Women's Institute. One of these is the bodily posture of the woman who, far from trying to flee the man's advances, arches her back, thereby moving her sex closer to him. Another detail is in the woman's face, desiring and not at all tense, which turns its gaze toward the young man dressed in blue at the far left of the picture, pointing him out as her next lover.

In this interpretation of the advertisement, one sees two different kinds of manipulative actions: The first is that exercised by the Woman's Institute, which used *intimidation* toward those aberrant readers of the advertisement, interpreting the perpetuation of the patriarchal gaze as a negative quality. The Women's Institute looked at the image created by Dolce & Gabbana in a patriarchal way, which neuters female desire if it does not conform to certain rules. These norms allow this desire to function so long as it is not a question of polygamous relationships or violence used as an erotic game, which is what the advertisement also appears to imply. The other form of manipulation is that of the ideas people in the Italian firm who used *provocation* to force readers accustomed to thinking about what lies behind this transgressive communicative act ("I want you to do this, and I contend that you are incapable of achieving it"), advocating sexual activity without any limits.

From childhood, women are warned of the dangers of being led by the pleasure principle, by their own pleasure. That is the argument of one of the most popular and repeated fairy tales during girls' childhood and adolescence: *Little Red Riding Hood*. The psychoanalyst Bruno Bettelheim believes that fairy tales help children to "master the psychological problems of growing up." Through the comprehensible situations presented in fairy tales, children learn to deal with their frustrations and complexes and to "relinquish childhood dependencies," gain a sense of "self-worth" and "selfhood," and "moral obligation" (Bettelheim 1991, 6) The Red Riding Hood of the protagonist in this celebrated tale symbolizes the young girl's incipient sexuality, a girl who has just entered adolescence after her first menstruation. According to Bettelheim, during puberty the girl's Oedipal desires toward her father are reactivated, and she develops a "fatal" fascination toward sex, which she experiences simultaneously with excitement and anxiety. However, Little Red Riding Hood is not yet a sexually mature woman who is capable of deciding whether it is appropriate to be driven by the desires that are just beginning to stir in her; or whether it would be better to follow the *principle of reality* that dictates the moral obligations of patriarchal society. In this sense,

> "Little Red Cap" externalizes the inner processes of the pubertal child: the wolf is the externalization of the badness the child feels when he goes contrary to the admonitions of his parents and permits himself to tempt, or to be tempted, sexually. When he strays from the path the parent has outlined for him, he encounters "badness," and he fears that it will swallow up him and the parent whose confidence he betrayed. (Bettelheim 1991, 177)

The moral, therefore, is clear: do not stray from the path that your mother has marked out for you or you will run the risk of being devoured by the wolf. "Deviating from the straight path in defiance of mother and superego was temporarily necessary for the young girl, to gain a higher state of personality organization. Her experience convinced her of the dangers of giving in to her oedipal desires. It is much better, she learns, not to rebel against the mother, nor try to seduce or permit herself to be seduced by the as yet dangerous aspects of the male" (Bettelheim 1991, 181). And Bettelheim is right. But it is no less true that this repression of instincts that is necessary for the correct education of the "I" has brought with it a reiterated denial and fear of expressing women's sexual desires; and all patriarchal graphic representations and traditional tales have only added to this and perpetuated it in an act of silent violence against female liberty.

In a sense, the words of Sigrid Weigel are still valid:

> Men are the first, the authentic sex. Women are always defined according to male criteria as regards their characteristics, behavior, etc. Woman in the male order has learnt to see herself as inferior, inauthentic and incomplete. As the cultural order is ruled by men but women still belong to it, women also use the norms of which they themselves are the object. That is, woman in the male order is once *involved* and *excluded*. This

means for woman's self-awareness that she sees herself by seeing *that* and *how* she is seen. She sees the world through male spectacles (The metaphor "spectacles" implies the utopia of a liberated, unhindered gaze.) She is fixated on self-observation refracted in the critical gaze of man, having left observation of the external world to his wide-ranging gaze. Thus her self-portrait originates in the distorting patriarchal mirror. In order to find her own image she must liberate the mirror from the *images of woman* painted on it by a male hand. (1986, 61)

Definitively, the patriarchy confines a system of invisibility on certain objects of value, exercising a manipulative process that can take on forms of temptation, seduction, intimidation, and provocation, in order to show itself and thereby shape a specific value system that might govern the behavior of contemporary women.

The patriarchy imposes certain canons of beauty on women under the promise of a positive sanction. That extreme visibility of the beautiful leads to a non-visually-representable world that shuts away ugliness and aging in media blindness, anchored in the terrain of nonexistence. Patriarchal culture condemns to the realm of the unseen both elderly bodies and sexual relations among senior citizens. In a similar way, it hides and banishes into limbo the existence of clitoral stimulation, excessively visualizing sexual relations based on male pleasure, and denying a specifically female sexuality, which is instead always directed toward pleasing men. Women manipulated by patriarchal society and its representatives, the media, must be beautiful and must seek pleasure through that of their male partners. Any other kinds of women continue to be, still now in the supposed era of female emancipation, material without visible form.

References

Alzon, Claude. 1982. *Mujer mitificada, mujer mistificada.* Translated by José Martín Arancibia. Barcelona: Ruedo Ibérico. French version: *Femme mythifiée, femme mystifiée.* Paris: Presses Universitaires de France, 1978.

Béjar, Sylvia de. 2009. *Tu sexo es aún más tuyo: Todo lo que has de saber para disfrutar de tu sexualidad.* Barcelona: Planeta.

Bettelheim, Bruno. 1991. *The Uses of Enchantment: The Meaning and Importance of Fairy Tales.* New York: Penguin. First published 1975.

Bornay, Erika. *Las hijas de Lilith.* 1995. Madrid: Cátedra.

Bouchard, Julie, and Pascal Froissart. 2004. "L'événement médiatique

Rapport Hite en 1976: Entretien avec Shere Hite." *MEI Médiation et information* 20: 7–12.

Courtine, Jean-Jacques. 2006. "El cuerpo anormal: Historia y antropología culturales de la deformidad." In *Historia del cuerpo*. Vol. 3, *Las mutaciones de la mirada: El siglo XX*, edited by Alain Corbin et al. Madrid: Santillana. French version: *Histoire du corps*. Paris: Seuil, 2005–6.

De Lauretis, Teresa. 1984. *Alice Doesn't: Feminism, Semiotics, Cinema*. Bloomington: Indiana University Press.

Greimas, Algirdas Julien, and Joseph Courtés. 1982. *Semiotics and Language: An Analytical Dictionary*. Translated by Larry Crist et al. Bloomington: Indiana University Press.

Hite, Shere. 1981. *The Hite Report on Male Sexuality*. New York: Knopf, distributed by Random House.

———. 2002. *El orgasmo femenino: Teorías sobre la sexualidad humana*. Barcelona: Ediciones B.

Kauffman, Linda S. 1998. *Bad Girls and Sick Boys: Fantasies in Contemporary Art and Culture*. Berkeley: University of California Press.

MacKinnon, Catharine A. 1982. "Feminism, Marxism, Method and the State: An Agenda for Theory." *Signs* 7, no. 3 (Spring): 515–44.

Merquior, José Guilherme. 1978. *La estética de Lévi-Strauss*. Translated by Antoni Vicens. Barcelona: Destino. French version: *L'Esthétique de Lévi-Strauss*. Paris: Presses Universitaires de France, 1977.

Paglia, Camille. 1990. *Sexual Personae: Art and Decadence from Nefertiti to Emily Dickinson*. New Haven, CT: Yale University Press.

Sontag, Susan. 1972. "The Double Standard of Aging." *Saturday Review of Literature* 39 (September 23): 29–38.

Weigel, Sigrid. 1986. "Double Focus: On the History of Women's Writing." In *Feminist Aesthetics*, edited by Gisela Ecker. Translated by Harriet Anderson. Boston: Beacon Press.

Wolf, Naomi. 1997. *Promiscuities: The Secret Struggle for Womanhood*. New York: Random House.

Young-Eisendrath, Polly. 1999. *Women and Desire: Beyond Wanting to Be Wanted*. New York: Harmony Books.

Zunzunegui, Santos. 1985. *Mirar la imagen*. Bilbao: Servicio Editorial de la Universidad del País Vasco/Euskal Herriko Unibertsitatea.

4

New Reference Points for Communicating Violent Conflicts: Poverty and Inequality and Positions in the Current Debate on the Causes of Civil Wars

Alfonso Dubois

Translated by Jennifer R. Ottman

Coverage of violent conflicts has been an area of interest for communication studies due to its overarching significance for both the perception of societies and their development, especially as a result of the media's creation of a favorable climate for conflict's outbreak and continuation. In recent decades, these conflicts, like the processes of poverty to which they are increasingly linked, have undergone profound changes in their origins and forms of manifestation, to the point that the representations that have been generally used to explain and communicate them no longer reflect their characteristics.

Among the movements that are raising questions about the role of the media in covering conflicts, special importance belongs to one that proposes the creation of a peace journalism in place of war journalism, with antecedents in Johan Galtung's proposal for a peace journalism in the 1970s. This idea acquired renewed impetus in the first decade of the twenty-first century and has given rise to an intense debate about how the function of the media and journalists can be understood in such a way that they can be a positive factor in peace building. Undoubtedly, it is easier to reach agreement on the negative aspects of conflict communication that need to be overcome than it is to formulate proposals for alternative forms of communication.

Another issue is the rethinking and redefinition of the journalist's role when faced with a conflict. Even if maximalist positions must be avoided, since it is not the media who start wars or determine how they end, journalists' growing influence on the processes of communication and social change is still beyond question. Concerned to find an alternative to conventional coverage, the peace-journalism movement[1] has driven the discussion from a normative perspective that holds that the media should play a positive role in promoting peace, but it has not united around a single proposal, and there are various currents within the movement regarding how that role should play out.[2]

The peace-journalism approach is a demonstration of the concern that exists among communications professionals about how conflicts should be covered. This chapter forms part of this line of reflection and seeks to contribute elements that can help to create more suitable communication about current wars. My objective is to identify the points of reference needed in order to understand these conflicts and develop a form of communication that can serve to better understand and publicize them, something that in itself constitutes a contribution to peace building. Specifically, this chapter proposes the necessity of understanding the links between poverty and conflict as a key element in providing that communication.

This chapter is divided into three parts. The first part lays out the current discussion about the existence of a causal relationship between civil war on the one hand and poverty and inequality on the other. The second addresses the recent linkage of global poverty with terrorism, a linkage that has modified national and international security strategies. The final section presents a case study analyzing the content and practices of communication among nongovernmental organizations in the Basque Country's development-cooperation sector.

---

1. For a general overview of the movement, see http://en.wikipedia.org/wiki/Peace_Journalism, and for a more specific introduction, www.peacejournalism.org/Welcome.html.

2. The electronic publication *Conflict & Communication Online* publishes research articles on peace journalism: www.cco.regener-online.de/. *Conflict & Communication Online* 6, no. 2 (2007), brings together a series of articles with various positions on how to understand an alternative journalism for peace.

Poverty and Inequality as Causal Factors in Conflicts

Until recently, poverty and conflict were studied separately. Poverty was considered solely in disciplines such as economics, anthropology, and sociology, and violent conflict fell under the area of expertise of political science, international relations, and peace and conflict studies. Recently, both processes have begun to be considered jointly, in a demonstration of how the changes evident in both have also had an impact on the nature of the relationship between them.

When addressing the links between violence and poverty, it is appropriate to consider numerous approaches, given the variety of situations and problems presented by their ties. We refer here to the relationship between violent conflict and poverty, understanding the former as the existence of a military conflict within a country or between several countries, taking the view that such a conflict exists when one thousand or more deaths occur per year as a result. Even if we limit ourselves to this kind of violence, it must be said that the differences among war, predatory violence, and crime are becoming ever more difficult to define (Goodhand 2001, 7). There are several reasons for our choice, but the fundamental one is the fact that the majority of current violent conflicts are taking place in countries that can be categorized as poor, something that, in turn, has led poverty to be included on the national-security agenda of more powerful countries.

Since the end of World War II, violent conflicts have gone from being wars between countries to wars within countries. The number of civil wars has increased. Likewise, these wars have become not only more frequent but also longer. The majority of conflicts today are prolonged civil wars. Both processes mark a significant change in the nature of war: victims of war today are more often found among people who dedicate themselves to productive activities than among those enlisted in armies or armed groups (Humphreys 2003).

The relationship between poverty and violent conflict can be viewed from two perspectives: one, poverty as a cause of conflict; and two, the effects of conflict on poverty. Although this second perspective may appear more obvious, current manifestations of violent conflict present novel situations of impoverishment, with particular severity and harmful effects for communities and individuals. In any event, it is the former aspect that has aroused more controversy.

The Debate on the Relationship between Poverty and Conflict

The interest in studying the links between poverty and violent conflict has arisen in recent years in response to the new characteristics manifested by wars, and debate about the nature of this relationship continues in full force. This concern is understandable in view of the evidence that the majority of current and recent wars have originated in circumstances marked by poverty and within a single country. Without going into detailed statistics, we can look briefly at three studies sufficient to demonstrate the importance and actuality of this phenomenon. Paul Collier (2007, 17) highlights the fact that of every one hundred inhabitants living in countries with severe poverty indicators, seventy-three have recently experienced a civil war or are currently suffering from one. For his part, Duncan Green (2008, 278) notes that from 1945 to 1989, more than one-third of conflicts took place in low-income developing countries, and since that date, their share has risen to more than one-half. The World Bank estimates the number of people living in fragile and conflict-affected countries at six hundred million.[3] Likewise, the bank emphasizes that one-fourth of states eligible to receive aid, that is, states characterized by their conditions of poverty, are immersed in conflict, and their poverty rates are much worse than those of the group of recipient countries as a whole. The World Bank does not assert that conflict occurs only in poor countries, but it cautions that, although violent conflict may not be limited to poor countries, a disproportionate number of conflicts take place in those countries.

Starting from these facts, the issue is whether it is possible to deduce the existence of a significant and demonstrable link between poverty and the risk that a country will fall into civil war. Research on this possible causal relationship between poverty and the outbreak of violent conflict has been conducted from two distinct perspectives. One is that of political economy, which grants special importance to economic factors and which considers it possible, on the basis of quantitative tools, to extract universal conclusions. The other, more multidimensional approach proposes that each scenario has its own characteristics and that it is not possible to deduce global results. Although this approach may include quantitative analysis, scholars in this group believe that it is necessary to understand each country's structural and historical factors in order to study these connections, and that it is not possible to establish universal conclusions.

---

3. See http://go.worldbank.org/BNFOS8V3S0.

The first approach takes the view that economic variables are significant conditioning factors for the outbreak of conflict, especially abrupt drops in economic activity and low income levels. Consequently, the idea is that the causes of violence are in some way rooted in poverty and inequality. The central thesis is that poor societies are more likely to fall into violent conflict than rich ones. These positions are chiefly based on the studies conducted by Paul Collier and colleagues (2003); Paul Collier, Anke Hoeffler, and Dominic Rohner (2009); and James D. Fearon and David D. Laitin (2003).[4]

Collier and Hoeffler (2004) empirically analyze the causes of civil war, comparing the list of civil conflicts with each country's socioeconomic data in order to determine which factors make the outbreak of war within the following five years more likely. According to their findings, the risk of war correlates with three factors: a country's initial income; slow growth, or even worse, negative growth or stagnation; and economic dependence on primary commodities. The conclusion is that the fundamental motivations for the outbreak of violent conflict are grievance (claims for redress by people who are experiencing severe fundamental lacks) and greed (the opportunities available for predatory accumulation by specific groups as a consequence of taking control of natural resources).[5] A relationship is ruled out between the risk of conflict and political repression, oppressed minorities, income inequality, ethnic conflicts, or previous colonization (Collier 2007, 18–26). A more recent study drawing on a wider range of data reaffirms the earlier conclusions. What is most notable is that the authors now add consideration of the feasibility of war to their proposal to study causality by starting from the motivations that can lead to war (grievance and greed). The feasibility hypothesis proposes that where rebellion is feasible, it will occur independent of any particular motivation (Collier, Hoeffler, and Rohner 2009). Collier's theses have been highly influential in political circles and have guided the cooperation policies of the major donor countries.

For their part, Fearon and Laitin (2003) agree with the previous authors that religious or ethnic diversity contributes very little to the risk of civil war and propose that the cause must be primarily sought in the

---

4. See Reynal-Querol (2009).

5. The most significant case may be the civil war in the Democratic Republic of the Congo, the location of 80 percent of the world's reserves of coltan, a mineral used in the high-tech industry.

weakening of state capacity in a context of poverty. The union of this thesis with that of Collier has led to an attractive and simple proposition: civil wars occur where there is devastating poverty and failed states characterized by inept, corrupt, and venal regimes, with war dynamics maintained by motivations similar to banditry. This perspective explains the inclusion of poverty on the security agenda of wealthier countries—something that, in its turn, makes it possible to put forward the possibility of intervention with the aim of preventing the collapse of fragile states (Murshed and Tadjoeddin 2009, 88). In fact, the preceding studies have served as a basis for various prominent political sectors to consider as proven the thesis that low-income countries have a greater risk of civil conflict, at the same time that the more widespread perception that conflict chiefly derives from cultural, religious, and ethnic factors is being overturned (Rice, Graff, and Lewis 2006).

Even supposing the existence of a positive correlation between civil conflict and impoverishment, however, can it be affirmed that the former is caused by the latter? One line of criticism questions the force of the theses that their backers consider proven, especially the causal foundation itself. The central argument of these critics is that we must break with that excessively simplistic and linear vision and open up the analytical framework in order to understand the complexity of the processes in question. Thus, Antonio Ciccone (2008) notes that there are good reasons to be cautious, since both poverty and conflict may be symptoms of other, broader political and social problems. For his part, Amartya Sen (2008) warns that making poverty responsible for group violence entails an excessive simplification of empirical connections and one that is far from universally applicable. The influence that inequality and poverty may have has to be understood as an exclusive focus on privation or misery at the margins of a society or culture, as well as by fitting them into a broader context in which poverty actively interacts with other aspects of society. Along the same lines, Ravi Kanbur (2007), while accepting that poverty and inequality promote conflict, maintains that it is not evident that clear and precise causal relationships exist.

Another line of criticism addresses the motivations taken into consideration in order to explain conflict outbreak. Once again, the critics point to the simplification entailed in proposing only grievance or greed as detonators. Many situations exist in which strong claims for redress are made or valuable natural resources are present without there being a risk of civil war. The presence of greed or grievance alone is not seen as sufficient. The decisive factor is that an institutional breakdown takes place—that is, that neither the state apparatus nor the mechanisms for participation or dispute resolution function, as Syed Mansoob Murshed and Mohammad Zulfan Tadjoedin (2009) indicate—in other words, a failure of the social contract occurs. Whether degradation of the social contract is more likely in a context of poverty or a situation of weak growth or stagnation is a different question. For other reasons, Jonathan Goodhand (2001) similarly disagrees with the importance assigned to grievance and greed, since in a situation of chronic poverty, it is unlikely that this in itself will lead to conflict. Nevertheless, social inequalities and social exclusion, especially when they coincide with group identities or regional borders, may increase that risk.

Within the analysis of the economic factors that may be causes of conflict, other variables to be taken into account have been proposed. For example, the possible significance of unforeseen and drastic events, such as a steep drop in economic activity or a natural disaster such as drought or flooding, has been analyzed. After examining conflicts in sub-Saharan Africa during the period from 1980 to 2006, Ciccone (2008) finds that conflict is much more likely to break out following a period of drought lasting several years, and that a 5 percent drop in income enormously increases the possibility of conflict.

Severe criticism has also been formulated from a methodological perspective. One of the most interesting contributions is the study by Simeon Djankov and Marta Reynal-Querol (2008), based on alternative data sources and developing samples of different durations over a retrospective time span of almost two hundred years, which questions previous results about poverty and civil war. Specifically, these authors do not find a strong association between the two once the possibility of a false correlation is taken into account.

Christopher Blattman and Edward Miguel (2009) have also expressed their disagreement with the majority of studies that, on the basis of econometric analysis, maintain that low per capita income, slow economic growth, and geographical conditions favor insurgency and that these are the factors most strongly associated with civil war. Their conclusions challenge those studies that use econometric methods. In the first place, they point out their weak theoretical foundation, since available theory about the origins of conflict is incomplete and the most significant theoretical proposals remain unproven. Second, even if these studies have up to now played an enormously provocative role, they have significant limitations, among which the authors note the following: (1) they rarely make a convincing causal identification of the key relationships, nor do they explore the solidity of alternative explanations; (2) country-years are considered as independent units in time and space; (3) the absence of evidence about specific effects has often been interpreted as evidence of absence; and (4) theories about the behavior of individuals or armed groups are verified at the country level, despite the obvious difficulties of aggregation. The authors propose the need to conduct micro-level analyses that can make it possible to decipher the causes of war and understand the behavior of armed groups.

Inequality as a Detonator of Conflict

The relationship between inequality and violent conflict has been a topic of interest in political economy. It seems reasonable to propose as a hypothesis that inequality fosters claims for redress; that the latter are more exigent in proportion to the acuteness of the former; that for that very reason, those claims become ever more difficult to satisfy; and that as a consequence, conditions result in which the outbreak of conflict can be expected.[6] Nevertheless, the real world offers many examples of societies with high levels of inequality in which we do not find open conflict expressed through violence. We should also not deduce from this that there is no link of any kind between the two, but should rather caution, as Sen (2008, 8–9) does, that connections should be made with care and always on the basis of empirical tests.

The introduction of inequality as a causal factor in conflict should not be understood as if it were a necessary or sufficient cause in itself; rather, its catalyzing function will depend on the particular characteristics with which it appears (Cramer 2005). In contrast, we must note the importance of ideology or of the theoretical presuppositions from which we start. The affirmations made about the links between economic inequality and violent political conflict are conditioned by the approach taken to understanding the origins of conflict and violence, even if they are not made explicit. Even the economic inequality that is being analyzed, even if it is limited to differences in income, will vary enormously according to the indicators used and the reference points adopted. The reality is that

---

6. The necessity of income redistribution is commonly justified, explicitly or implicitly, with the argument that excessive inequality threatens social cohesion and may provoke situations of open conflict.

quantitative analyses do not lead to satisfactory conclusions, thereby leaving enormous uncertainty about the links between economic inequality and violent political conflict. Christopher Cramer (2005) has highlighted the empirical deficiencies to be found in the great majority of affirmations made in this regard.

A novel proposal for considering the relationship between inequality and conflict is the one put forward by the Centre for Research on Inequality, Human Security and Ethnicity (CRISE) research project, led by Frances Stewart (Stewart, Brown, and Langer 2007). The reference point for this analysis is a specific modality of inequality: horizontal inequality. Horizontal inequalities are inequalities among groups and may have various social, political, economic, and other dimensions. The point of departure is the argument that horizontal inequalities constitute the manifestation of inequality with the greatest potential to impact a conflict, an aspect to which the international community has not paid attention until now.

In a recent study, these scholars analyze the correlation between horizontal inequalities and conflict in eight countries, finding that when those inequalities are severe, they can be a significant source of conflict, especially if they are consistent across several dimensions (Stewart 2010). While socioeconomic inequalities generally prepare the ground for conflict, and cultural inequalities act to unite groups, horizontal inequalities offer leaders incentives to mobilize their people to rebel. In conditions of profound horizontal inequality, if abrupt changes occur in political horizontal inequalities, or cultural incidents in which important cultural or religious symbols are attacked, these events can often be powerful detonators of conflict.

The study concludes by proposing as plausible hypotheses that conflict is more likely to occur where economic or political horizontal inequalities are significant, that political mobilization is more likely where existing horizontal inequalities are consistent with one another, and that cultural recognition and status inequalities are also provocative elements. Other factors also exist that play a significant role in whether conflict occurs, such as the nature of the state and its reactions, the role of local institutions in pacifying or exacerbating a conflict once it has begun, and the presence of natural resources, due to their impact on horizontal inequalities (Stewart 2010, 300). This focus on horizontal inequalities has received widespread favorable attention for overcoming the simplistic approaches of previous studies and offering a multidisciplinary framework that takes into account the specific realities of each case.

Poverty and Security

Until recently, although voices were occasionally heard warning about the threat poverty might pose to international stability, it was not considered a security concern, with the consequence that it never became part of security strategies.

The current view of security pays specific and growing attention to the social crises that appear on the world stage. The meaning of state security has been the object of revision, on the understanding that global poverty is a threat because of its incidence in provoking significant social crises: environmental disasters, famines, mass unemployment, migration, the spread of disease, and so on.

Likewise, the failure of numerous states to fulfill the functions of control of their territory or of the use of violence, especially starting in the twentieth century's last decade, has favored not only the intensification of civil wars, humanitarian disasters, and displaced populations but also a boom in hidden economies and the strengthening of powerful nonstate actors, such as the global black market and organized-crime and terrorist networks. The connection between poverty and security thus makes ever more frequent appearances in the reports of international organizations, and it has become a commonplace to affirm the existence of a profound relationship between poverty reduction and global security.

This perception is widely endorsed at present, and a current of opinion linking poverty and security is consolidating, especially in sectors of the US administration (Brainard and Chollet 2007; Rice, Graff, and Pascual 2010). This perspective has significant consequences in the way it approaches the fight against poverty, which can no longer be considered independent of security considerations. If poverty is conducive to insecurity on a global scale, the motivation to fight poverty is not only found in the moral imperative that arises from suffering and the denial of opportunities for basic human fulfillment; it is also rooted in the need to guarantee international order and peace. Moreover, these latter goals are more urgent and powerful. On the international level, the G8 summit held in Gleneagles, Scotland, in 2005 reinforced the approach linking poverty with security when it proclaimed the importance of the fight against poverty for global stability.

In particular, the US representative to the United Nations, Susan E. Rice, has defended the thesis of the relationship between poverty and national security. This is a thesis that was already found in the 2002

National Security Strategy, under the preceding Bush administration, which indicated that while poor people may not be terrorists, poverty in conjunction with fragile states forms a breeding ground for terrorism and drug trafficking (Tortosa 2006). In Rice's (2010) understanding, a paradigm shift has taken place since the Cold War in how international security is understood. The threat of nuclear war has disappeared, but the danger of conflict around the world has not gone away. Now, the threats have different origins, and their consequences are more diffuse. It is no longer hostile states that attract security attention but rather transnational threats such as terrorism, weapons proliferation, the global economic crisis, infectious diseases, drug trafficking and international crime, climate change, and environmental degradation. These threats may take very diverse forms, depending on a variety of factors, but the author considers that state weaknesses play a role in the ways in which they manifest.

Those who defend the inclusion of poverty on the security agenda find their arguments in the results of Collier and other academics' empirical research (e.g., Brainard and Chollet 2007; Rice, Graff, and Lewis 2006). At the same time, they grant special significance to the category of weak, fragile, and failed states that may become high-risk areas in a globalized world. The threats of conflict, terrorism, contagious diseases, and environmental degradation are strengthened by the existence of these states, which constitute an ideal platform for encouraging and fostering them. Hence, another way of viewing the relationship between poverty and conflict is to analyze that relationship from the perspective of failed, fragile, or weak states, in accordance with the various labels. In other words, it is a matter of determining whether those states that are poor not only due to their meager economic results but also due to the weakness of their institutions is a risk factor for conflict.

This proposal has been widely discussed, and the fragility or weakness of states is spoken of as if these were clearly defined and widely accepted terms. Nevertheless, the reality is very far from this supposed consensus. Rather, there has been a proliferation of definitions of fragility, as Marta Reynal-Querol (2009) indicates. Among these, the following may be mentioned: The Department for International Development (DFID)[7] considers those countries in which governments are unable or unwilling to provide basic services to the majority of the population,

---

7. The official United Kingdom government agency for development cooperation.

including the poor, to be fragile states; the United States Agency for International Development (USAID)[8] differentiates between vulnerable states and states in crisis; and the journal *Foreign Policy* considers countries that have lost physical control of their territory or have lost their monopoly on the legitimate use of force to be failed states and looks to other attributes to characterize fragile states.[9] International organizations also have their own categories, as in the case of the World Bank, which considers low-income countries with a rating of 3.2 or less on the Country Policy and Institutional Assessment (CPIA) to be fragile states, with the result that it classified forty-five countries under that heading in 2005.[10] In addition, the need to apply the label of "fragile state" is highly controversial, on the view that it corresponds to specific interests that obscure the complex reality of those countries, which by the mere fact of receiving that categorization become targets of suspicion and objects of security attention, while their status as developing countries in need of collaboration to overcome their situation is relegated to a subordinate plane.

In any event, the concept of fragility is linked to the inability or unwillingness of governments to provide services to their citizens, even if this last specification is much more debated. The majority of definitions suggest that fragility has to do with the lack or weakness of institutional capabilities. It is from this starting point that the link between fragile states, on the one hand, and conflict and terrorism, on the other, is established, insofar as they provide the conditions for violent extremist organizations to take up residence.

The majority of terrorism experts maintain that empirical evidence does not allow us to affirm that poverty is correlated with a higher incidence of terrorism. In addition to this lack of empirical evidence, specific studies exist that deny this link. For example, a well-known study by Alan B. Krueger and Jitka Malecková (2003) concludes that there is scarcely any direct connection among poverty, education, and participation in ter-

---

8. The official United States government agency for development cooperation.

9. Study conducted by the Fund for Peace: www.fundforpeace.org.

10. See the World Bank website, http://go.worldbank.org/4RID3HUNW0. Countries with a CPIA below 3.0 are considered "core" fragile states, and those with a CPIA between 3.0 and 3.2 are considered "marginal" fragile states. The CPIA scores are used to evaluate a country's institutional framework and policies, although the bank itself warns that they depict the "spectrum" of fragility and should not be interpreted as strict standards. In other words, countries with a CPIA below 3.2 might not demonstrate fragility, and others with a score above 3.2 might in fact do so.

rorism. In fact, according to available data, the majority of militants in various revolutionary movements come from families with a comfortable financial position and a high level of education. Safiya Aftab (2008) has examined possible ties between the incidence of poverty and radicalization or increased militancy in Pakistan. The data on the spatial distribution of poverty do not suggest that poverty is to be found, or is above average, in areas characterized by intense militant activity. There is little evidence to support the idea that poverty in itself feeds extremism.

However, this conclusion does not seem convincing to some political sectors. For Rice (2010), the affirmations by academics that poverty is not a cause of terrorism are superficial and mistaken. Even assuming that they may be correct on an individual level, she asks whether global poverty has no repercussions for the security of the United States. Along these lines, Corinne Graff (2010), in view of the persistence of terrorist activity in countries such as Yemen, investigates the conditions that enable violent extremists to operate, obtain support, and recruit individuals. On the one hand, she believes that denial of the linkage between poverty and terrorism has been accepted by certain academic circles without submitting it to scrupulous analysis and that it has been based on a simplistic conception of violent extremism. For that reason, she believes that its results are not conclusive. On the other hand, she maintains that this vision changes when we look at what is happening on the ground. Even if there may not be any empirical evidence of a causal relationship between poverty and terrorist attacks, she believes that there is in fact new evidence that fragile and failed states, the majority of which are extremely poor, pose a growing risk of hosting violent extremism. She emphasizes that there are countries, such as Yemen, in which young people do not have a future, and fanatics offer them the dream that it is possible to take power and thereby overturn that situation. At the same time, poverty weakens government capacity and enables violent extremists to make use of those ungoverned territories by turning them into bases for their activities. Moreover, during the most recent period, no terrorist attacks have occurred in countries in which poverty, lack of job opportunities, or insufficient state capacity were not present. In her view, there is empirical evidence to maintain that a state's fragility is a predictive indicator for international terrorism, since those countries classified as at greatest risk of becoming failed states, according to the Fund for Peace's Failed Status Index, are three times more likely to suffer an attack than those in the two stronger categories. Although a causal relationship cannot be deduced from this, she maintains that reality contradicts the expert consensus and that, despite the many statements made pointing in the opposite direction, there is little evidence to suggest that poverty does not affect the incidence of terrorist attacks. In the end, the quantitative studies that deny that relationship are a poor guide for policy, while the increasing evidence that fragile states are vulnerable to violent extremism is more convincing.

To summarize, the thesis is that global poverty is a threat, one that is ceasing to be a merely humanitarian concern and is becoming, over the long term, a process that could threaten US national security. In the twenty-first century, poverty must be considered a significant conduit for transnational threats.

The overarching significance of accepting this vision of poverty marked by security concerns is evident in the proposals made to the governments of poor countries. These proposals are based on the individual geostrategic interests of particular countries that put forward containment measures to eliminate possible centers of instability, without resolving the underlying issues of poverty and inequality. Security now has absolute priority over any other decision-making criterion, and even development aid is subordinated to the so-called war on terror (Tortosa 2006). The use of the fight against poverty as a facade or justification for attaining other objectives in the area of national security is one of the chief consequences of this approach. A new factor is thereby introduced: one that weakens development priorities by elevating the global war on terror, the spatial confines of which are never clearly defined. This makes evident the decisive importance of the theory adopted about the causes of conflict.

Simplification in the effort to determine the causal relationship between poverty and conflict is the chief criticism that can appropriately be made of these approaches. While it is true that war, like other forms of violence, has a problematic relationship with poverty and inequality, it is not appropriate to deduce that the latter causes the former, even if inequality may provide favorable conditions for poverty's outbreak. The connections are not always linear or even clear, in many cases due to the analyst's desire to find what he or she wants to find, based more on policies that have already been decided than on the concrete analysis of specific situations.

I agree with Huma Haider's (2009, 5) synthesis of the causes of conflict, made following an extensive review of the recent literature, which states: There is no single cause of conflict. On the contrary, conflict is multidimensional and multicausal and depends on the specific context in which it originates. There may be a combination of the following: political and institutional factors such as weak state institutions, power struggles among elites and political exclusion, breakdown of the social contract and corruption, and identity politics; socioeconomic factors such as inequality, exclusion, and marginalization, absent or weak social cohesion, and poverty; and environmental resource factors such as greed, scarcity of national resources, often as a consequence of demographic growth leading to environmental insecurity, and unjust resource exploitation. Each of these factors may be a cause, a dynamic, or an impact of conflict. Identifying and understanding the interactions among the several causes, dimensions, and dynamics of conflict, and the particular contexts within which they arise, is essential in order to determine the potential areas for intervention and to design the appropriate approaches and methods for conflict transformation, resolution, and prevention. The way in which a government or institution, on the international or local level, addresses conflict can determine whether the parties will resort to conflict or will resolve their disputes through negotiation.

A Case Study: Communicating Conflict from the Perspective of Nongovernmental Organizations in the Basque Country[11]

There are two reasons for including this case study. One is to break with a vision that is blind to the existence of other communication agents beyond the conventional media. Even if nongovernmental organizations focusing on development cooperation may not constitute powerful actors, their work, which has achieved noteworthy results on occasion, should not be undervalued. The second reason is to overcome the perception of distance that exists with regard to major international issues, as if they were always resolved in transnational spaces in which local societies have nothing to contribute. Any conflict, however distant it may be, affects all communities. Moreover, the resolution, exacerbation, or persistence of a conflict depends to a great degree on how it is perceived and what reactions it receives. Shaping public opinion in each society matters and is decisive for a pacification strategy. For this reason, I will now examine how that alternative communication process is occurring in the Basque Country.

---

11. The work done by Andrea Cosson Gerstl, a student in the master's degree program in development and cooperation at the Instituto Hegoa, Universidad del País Vasco/Euskal Herriko Unibertsitatea (University of the Basque Country, UPV/EHU), has been indispensable to the conduct of this study.

In general, nongovernmental organizations have always considered raising awareness and development education among their core functions in relation to the societies in which they have their roots. These functions focus on publicizing the reality experienced by impoverished countries and, in particular, on offering another kind of information about violent conflicts on the ground than that provided by conventional media. The content and the tools that they have used have not always been the same. In a first stage, these organizations' concerns were rooted in collecting funds to alleviate the disasters of war, and their communication strategies therefore sought to be as explicit as possible in showing the severity of Third World armed conflicts, so as to demonstrate the urgency of collaborating to alleviate their harsh consequences. This resulted in the dissemination of an image of the countries of the global South, characterized by aspects of destruction and barbarism, which was of little help in understanding the underlying causes of conflict.

Progressively, the organizations' perception of the development problems matured, as the discussion about the concept of development evolved to consider dimensions other than economic growth alone, thereby changing their policies toward raising awareness. Their objectives became more ambitious, such as helping to decipher the origins of problems, awakening a critical consciousness among citizens, and generating practices of solidarity and active commitment. In the specific case of the relationship between violent conflict and poverty, the various approaches have focused on learning about its causes and consequences from a multidisciplinary perspective that avoids analyzing it as a problem taken in isolation from the affected population, which, in addition, includes other decisive variables that have more to do with the international community's behavior.

In the case of the Basque Country, nongovernmental organizations have also participated in this evolution in approaches to raising awareness and development education. On the local level, they have played an active role in offering Basque society a vision of the conflicts in the countries of the global South from a more open perspective and one independent of strategic and economic interests. The objective of this case study was to determine to what extent these organizations' activities directed toward raising awareness take into account the indicated points of reference for current conflicts. For this purpose, the object of study was defined as the fifty organizations with a website registered with the Basque Development NGO Coordinator (Coordinadora de ONGD de Euskadi),[12] leaving out those without a website on the view that this is a basic indicator of their degree of involvement in the function of raising awareness. The differences in these organizations' size and, consequently, in the resources available to them, made it impossible to deduce meaningful aggregate conclusions. For that reason, the case study limited itself to highlighting these organizations' main publicity messages that demonstrated a meaningful capacity for action and a high level of commitment and dedication to raising awareness specifically about violence and conflict in impoverished countries.

Accordingly, the case study analyzed the themes of twelve organizations' messages. A first sketch of the chief areas of their content devoted to raising awareness allowed the study to note that a significant part makes reference to the serious situation arising from the existence of conflict, but also—and this is important to emphasize—to creating a culture of peace, opening discussion about the ways in which conflicts can be avoided or proposing solutions. The activities that serve as channels for raising awareness can be grouped into the following categories: campaigns, publications, and educational programs.

Campaigns

Of the twelve organizations selected, five of them have created powerful communications campaigns in the past ten years—that is, interventions entailing a set of actions over an extended period and with the objective of reaching the majority of Basque society. The most widely publicized issues have been those related to the situation of child soldiers, arms control, the ravages of antipersonnel mines, and a culture that promotes peace. Their primary objective was political pressure through public statements and raising awareness among the Basque population about the contribution or co-responsibility of the states and societies of the global North in the prevalence of these situations. In their majority, these campaigns took a global approach, providing aggregate data about the consequences suffered by societies during and after conflict, without considering specific countries. Other issues that have been the target of campaigns have included the conflicts in Palestine and the Congo and the particular situation of women as victims of war.

---

12. See www.ongdeuskadi.org.

Publications

All the organizations selected have publications that discuss armed conflicts. Unlike the awareness-raising campaigns, the publications have more specific content with regard to particular areas in conflict: Colombia, Palestine, Western Sahara, Afghanistan, Sudan, the Democratic Republic of the Congo, Guatemala, and Chiapas. The content reflects a concern to take a position in favor of individuals or groups considered victims of injustice. Hence, the organizations criticize, when appropriate, the governments of the countries in conflict, but they also assign responsibility to the management of large transnational firms as generators of conflict in certain communities. Several publications make visible how internal armed conflicts affect men and women differently, with special emphasis on sexual violence, particularly rape, of which women are the victims, especially in countries such as Guatemala, Peru, and Colombia. The case of indigenous women as victims of political violence on the part of illegal armed groups and their countries' police and armed forces is highlighted. More generally, there are publications that discuss human-rights violations, unfinished peace processes, and the community's role in conflict situations. One of the organizations, active throughout Spain but with a publication program explicitly targeting the Basque Country, stands out for publications with greater analytical ambition that study the causes of conflicts and ways to address violence in impoverished countries and that harshly criticize international organizations such as the United Nations, the incoherence of international diplomacy; the price of peace versus the human, gender, environmental, and economic cost of war; the military-industrial complex; and the arms trade.

Special Events and Educational Programs

A variety of exhibits have been mounted in public spaces on topics such as life despite war in the Ivory Coast, the persistence of human-rights violations in Colombia and Palestine, and refugees and displaced people, but activities of this kind have not been the most prominent in the area of raising awareness. In contrast, even though they are addressed to small groups, it is worth highlighting the organization of specific workshops on war-related issues, among which the case study notes two recent ones that demonstrate the areas of greatest concern: (1) communication, conflicts, and human rights: the role of and the tools available to social movements and development organizations, posing the question of the extent to which development nongovernmental organizations and social movements can contribute through communication to achieving more just, egalitarian, and sustainable societies; and (2) women in conflict situations: reflections along feminist lines, pursuing an area of priority interest in all activities.

It is impossible to evaluate the impact that these activities have had. On the basis of this analysis, however, it is possible to identify a series of trends that characterize the awareness-raising message: the organizations take an attitude of denunciation with regard to the actors who produce violence, in response to conflict situations in countries in which they have development projects; they are concerned to offer a multidimensional perspective on the reality of those countries, from the standpoint of those on the bottom of the social pyramid looking up, and not the reverse, giving voice to those who are disadvantaged and not to the opinion of the organization from the global North; and they present a powerful gender perspective, both in campaigns and in awareness-raising activities, one of the manifestations of which is the analysis of new facets of violence generated by conflict, such as sexual violence as a weapon of war or feminicide. In summary, nongovernmental organizations, within their limits, accept their role as agents of communication and demonstrate in their messages a vision of war that is coherent with the new manifestations of that phenomenon.

References

Aftab, Safiya. 2008. "Poverty and Militancy." *Pips Journal of Conflict and Peace Studies* 1, no. 1 (October–December): 65–86. Accessed January 17, 2012. www.humansecuritygateway.com/documents/PIPS_PovertyAndMilitancy.pdf.

Blattman, Christopher, and Edward Miguel. 2009. "Civil War." NBER Working Paper No. 14801 (March), National Bureau of Economic Research, Cambridge, MA.

Brainard, Lael, and Derek H. Chollet, eds. 2007. *Too Poor for Peace? Global Poverty, Conflict, and Security in the 21st Century*. New York: Brookings Institutions Press. Accessed January 17, 2012. www.cco.regener-online.de.

Ciccone, Antonio. 2008. "Transitory Economic Shocks and Civil Conflict." CEPR Discussion Paper No. 7081 (December), Centre for Economic Policy Research, London.

Collier, Paul. 2007. *The Bottom Billion: Why the Poorest Countries Are Failing and What Can Be Done About It*. Oxford: Oxford University Press.

Collier, Paul, and Anke Hoeffler. 2004. "Greed and Grievance in Civil War." *Oxford Economic Papers* 56, no. 4: 563–95.

Collier, Paul, Anke Hoeffler, and Dominic Rohner. 2009. "Beyond Greed and Grievance: Feasibility and Civil War." *Oxford Economic Papers* 61, no. 1: 1–27.

Collier, Paul, Lani Elliott, Håvard Hegre, Anke Hoeffler, Marta Reynal-Querol, and Nicholas Sambanis. 2003. *Breaking the Conflict Trap: Civil War and Development Policy*. Washington, DC: The World Bank and Oxford University Press.

Cramer, Christopher. 2005. "Inequality and Conflict: A Review of an Age-Old Concern." Identities, Conflict, and Cohesion: Programme Paper No. 11 (October), UN Research Institute for Social Development, Geneva.

Djankov, Simeon, and Marta Reynal-Querol. 2008. "Poverty and Civil War: Revisiting the Evidence." CEPR Discussion Paper No. 6980 (July), Centre for Economic Policy Research, London. Accessed January 17, 2012. www.cepr.org/pubs/new-dps/showdp.asp?dpno=6980.

Fearon, James D., and David D. Laitin. 2003. "Ethnicity, Insurgency, and Civil War." *American Political Science Review* 97, no. 1: 75–90.

Goodhand, Jonathan. 2001. "Violent Conflict, Poverty, and Chronic Poverty." CPRC Working Paper No. 6, Chronic Poverty Research Centre, London.

Graff, Corinne. 2010. "Poverty, Development, and Violent Extremism in Weak States." In *Confronting Poverty: Weak States and US National Security*, edited by Susan E. Rice, Corinne Graff, and Carlos Pascual. New York: Brookings Institution Press.

Green, Duncan. 2008. *From Poverty to Power: How Active Citizens and Effective States Can Change the World*. Oxford, UK: Oxfam International.

Haider, Huma. 2009. *Topic Guide on Conflict*. London: Governance and Social Development Resource Centre, Department for International Development. Accessed January 17, 2012. www.gsdrc.org.

Humphreys, Macartan. 2002. "Economics and Violent Conflict." Program on Humanitarian Policy and Conflict Research, Harvard University. Accessed January 17, 2012. www.unglobalcompact.org/docs/issues_doc/Peace_and_Business/Economics_and_Violent_Conflict.pdf.

Kanbur, Ravi. 2007. "Poverty and Conflict: The Inequality Link." Coping with Crisis Working Paper Series (June), International Peace Institute, New York. Accessed January 17, 2012. www.ipinst.org.

Krueger, Alan B., and Jitka Malecková. 2003. "Education, Poverty and Terrorism: Is There a Causal Connection?" *Journal of Economic Perspectives* 17, no. 4 (Fall): 119–44.

Murshed, Syed Mansoob, and Mohammad Zulfan Tadjoeddin. 2009. "Revisiting the Greed and Grievance: Explanation for Violent Internal Conflict." *Journal of International Development* 21: 87–111.

Reynal-Querol, Marta. 2009. "Brief Survey on Fragility, Conflict, Aid Effectiveness and Aid in Fragile Countries." Accessed January 17, 2012. http://erd.eui.eu/media/survey-by-reynal-querol.pdf.

Rice, Susan E. 2006. "Global Poverty, Weak States and Insecurity." Paper presented at the Brookings Blum Roundtable, Aspen, CO, August 2. Accessed March 14, 2012. www.brookings.edu/papers/2006/08globaleconomics_rice.aspx.

———. 2010. "The National Security Implications of Global Poverty." In *Confronting Poverty: Weak States and US National Security*, edited by Susan E. Rice, Corinne Graff, and Carlos Pascual. New York: Brookings Institution Press.

Rice, Susan E., Corinne Graff, and Janet Lewis. 2006. "Poverty and Civil War: What Policymakers Need to Know." Global Economy and Development Working Paper No. 2 (December), Brookings Institution, New York.

Rice, Susan E., Corinne Graff, and Carlos Pascual, eds. 2010. *Confronting Poverty: Weak States and US National Security*. New York: Brookings Institution Press.

Sen, Amartya. 2008. "Violence, Identity and Poverty." *Journal of Peace Research* 45, no.1: 5–15.

Stewart, Frances, ed. 2010. *Horizontal Inequalities and Conflict: Understanding Group Violence in Multiethnic Societies*. Foreword by Kofi Annan. Basingstoke, UK: Palgrave, MacMillan.

Stewart, Frances, Graham Brown, and Arnim Langer. 2007. "Policies towards Horizontal Inequalities." Crise Working Paper No. 42 (March), Department of International Development (Queen Elizabeth House), University of Oxford, Oxford, UK. Accessed January 17, 2012. www.crise.ox.ac.uk/.

Tortosa, José María. 2006. "Ciudadanía, desarrollo y violencia: Algunas conexiones." Grupo de Estudios de Paz y Desarrollo, Universidad de Alicante. Accessed January 17, 2012. http://rua.ua.es/dspace/bitstream/10045/2883/1/ciudadaniayviolencia.pdf.

5

Violence and the Internet: New Technologies, Old Problems

MAIALEN GARMENDIA, CARMELO GARITAONANDIA, GEMMA
MARTÍNEZ, and MIGUEL ÁNGEL CASADO

Translated by Julie Waddington

The growth of the Internet has brought numerous changes and social transformations. The networks have brought about a new society, and the Internet has gone from being a tool to being the central axis of this new society model. In the words of Manuel Castells (2010, 508), "Information is the key ingredient of our social organization and why flows of messages and images between networks constitute the basic thread of our social organization." One of the characteristics of this social model, governed by technological advances, is that these advances often occur over and above advances in society. This new situation has resulted in countless adjustment problems associated with social and individual behavior, as well as the capacity to regulate the new information and communication technologies (ICTs).

With regards to the Internet in particular, these aspects have generated serious concerns about the emergence of spaces or activities on the Net that may generate more violence or, in the opinion of some, the degradation of society's moral values. The idea of an Internet that is "out of control," outside the law or any other kind of regulation, has taken root in many spheres.

Within this environment, particular alarm has been generated around the most "vulnerable" groups' uses of the Internet, focusing most of the attention on young people. There has, therefore, been considerable research carried out on the relation young people maintain with new technologies. Much early research focused on young people's video game habits, and on the negative influence that the violent content of some of these interfaces may have on the young person. Today, with Internet consumption being widespread among European youngsters,[1] research attention is focused on the different ways in which they use the Net and the risks involved in these practices. The research work of EU Kids Online[2] can also be found within this sphere. Although, in this particular case, this network's research aims to go beyond the question of the risks that young people may encounter on the Net in order to carry out a more thorough study that covers young people's general relation with the Internet, considering both the risks as well as the countless beneficial opportunities.

The conceptual framework in which EU Kids Online research is conducted is based on a classification of risks and opportunities that the Internet presents for minors, and its approach is therefore focused on the following three Cs: content, contact, and conduct. This classification stems from the three communication modes that the Internet enables: *content*, from one specific source to many sources (the minor as the recipient of content distributed on a mass scale); *contact*, from an adult to a minor (the minor as participant in an interactive situation fundamentally directed by the adult); and *conduct*, among equals (the minor as actor in an interaction in which he or she may be the initiator or perpetrator).

According to these three modes of communication, minors may find four main risk factors that may affect their development and well-being (commercial, aggressive, sexual, related to values) and four main categories of online opportunities: education and learning; participation and

---

1. According to the Eurobarometer of 2008, the percentage of young European individuals between six and seventeen who used the Internet was 75 percent. However, there are still differences between countries that may oscillate between 91 percent consumption in Sweden, or 93 percent in Holland, and 50 percent in Greece or Cyprus.

2. EU Kids Online is a European research network financed by the Safer Internet Plus program of the European Commission. It developed the second phase of its work in the period 2009–2011, with the participation of twenty-five European countries and nearly one hundred researchers. During this second phase of the project, the widest-ever survey carried out in Europe on the use that parents and children make of the Internet was conducted in order to develop a series of political recommendations aimed at the European Commission. www.lse.ac.uk/collections/EUKidsOnline/.

civic engagement; creativity; and identity and social connection (Hase-brink et al. 2007).

Table 5.1. Classification of risks and opportunities on the net for minors

		Content: The child as recipient	Contact: The child as participant	Conduct: The child as actor
Oppor-tunities	**Learning, digital skills and knowledge**	Educational resources	Contact with other children who share the same interests	Learning on their own initiative or with others
	Participation and social commitment	Global information	Exchanges with other special interest groups	Specific forms of social participation
	Creativity and expression	Wealth of resources	Being invited or inspired to create or participate	Content creator
	Identity and social connection	Recommendations (e.g., personal, health, sexuality)	Participate in social networks, share experiences with others	Expression of the person's own identity
Risks	**Commercial**	Publicity, spam, sponsors	Be observed or have personal information collected	Bets, illegal downloads, hacking
	Aggressive	Violent, bloody, or aggressive content	Be victimized, harassed or hounded	Victimize or harass others
	Sexual	Harmful pornographic and/or sexual content	Meet strangers, be the victim of grooming	Create and/or upload pornographic material on the Net
	Values	Racism, spurious information and suggestions	Inflict damage on oneself, be the victim of undesirable suggestions	Give advice, e.g. Suicide / pro anorexia.

Source: Livingstone y Haddon (2009), 10.

In most cases, the Internet's risks or negative aspects obfuscate the positive aspects and the possibilities that they offer for young people's development. In this sense, many researchers have drawn attention to the need to consider these opportunities in order to ensure that young people make the best use of the Internet. Sonia Livingstone and Ellen Helsper (2007) examine the idea of a ladder or range of opportunities that has become a common denominator for many European researchers and that reflects the way in which young people gradually discover Internet opportunities. This ladder of opportunities can be summed up in the following steps (Livingstone and Helsper 2007, 683–84):

- Step 1 centers on information seeking. This is the first step for everyone and characterizes Internet use among those who just take up a few online opportunities. They may be termed *basic users.*
- Step 2 adds in games and e-mail. Those who take up a few more opportunities are more likely to use the Internet for information, entertainment, and communication. They may be termed *moderate users.*
- Step 3 adds in instant messaging and downloading music. Those who take up still more opportunities, continue to seek information, and also expand their peer-to-peer engagement. They may be termed *expert users.*
- Step 4 adds in a wide range of interactive and creative uses. Those who make the most use of the opportunities on the Internet. They may be termed *all-rounders.*

Risks Associated with New Technologies

Different developments and technological advances have always brought with them fears and mistrust for some sectors of society, who consider their influence to be potentially negative, particularly in terms of aspects relating to the maintenance of social order and morals. These fears have been particularly pronounced in the case of advances based on the reproduction, coordination, and dissemination of *information*, such as in the case of television and video games. Nowadays, the state of convergence and multidimensionality of information technologies means that these fears have been fueled further (Sandywell 2006, 41), with the Internet being their focal point.

One of the ways of evaluating this reaction to the influence of technology is to analyze the way the media deals with this phenomenon, examining which aspects have been covered, what overall view is offered of the phenomenon, and which sources have been consulted in the preparation of the news items.

Various studies have taken this line of questioning. A study by Jaime Ridell in 1995 indicates that 40 percent of the press articles studied contained misleading statistics and concludes that British newspapers exaggerated the dangers of the Internet in order to imply that the medium was "out of control" (Riddell 1995, in Littlewood 2003, 10).

Anne Littlewood (2003) also carried out a study of the British media's coverage of the Internet between 1995 and 1999.[3] Of all the articles analyzed, 63 percent of them revealed unfavorable coverage of the Internet, only 13 percent showed favorable coverage, and 12 percent showed both sides of the Internet. The study also indicated expressions that were linked to the Internet—"obscene," "illegal," "perversion"—and which showed a negative side to it. In this case, most of the negative Internet references focused on pornography, whose presence on the Internet, according to Littlewood, was over-represented giving the medium a distorted image.

In this sense, it is important to take into account that these studies, carried out at the end of the nineties, are based on a reality of the Internet that is substantially different to the current one. At that time, the main causes for concern about the Internet were those related to inappropriate content, whether violent or pornographic. Today, the reality of the Internet after the Web 2.0 evolution is another one altogether. The fears, and what we could call the moral panics, relate, above all, to the possibility of adults harassing children through social networks and so on: the possibility of *grooming*—deliberately befriending a child to lure them into sexual or other exploitation—or even harassment among the young people themselves, as is the case with cyberbullying. In this sense, the fears associated with the Internet have evolved alongside the evolution of the Net itself.

These perceptions should not, however, be generalized, as, for example, the study by Patrick Rössler (2001) on the way that German magazines treated the Internet on similar dates, shows very different results. This study shows that the presence of positive elements is greater in forms of press that are fundamentally supported by economic factors and market opportunities arising from the Internet.

Another study carried out in Spain, and focused on audiovisual media, indicates that almost a third of the news items related to the Internet shown on the main channels (TV1, A3, T5, and C+) were negative, with 20 percent being alarmist. By contrast, according to the same study, the information given on the radio is more balanced, taking in all perspectives of the Net (AccesoMetrix 2003).

---

3. The media included in the study included the *Times*, the *Guardian*, and the *Daily Telegraph*, and the tabloids the *Daily Mail* and the *Mirror*.

Minors and the Internet: Real Fears, Unfounded Fears, and Opportunities

In the specific case of the relation between young people and communication technologies, the diffusion of this negative Internet image is one of the factors that can have the most influence on parents' perceptions of the Net and, consequently, may be a factor that conditions the mediation between parents and children in the correct use of it. Three main aspects generate concern among parents regarding minors' use of the Internet:

- The extraordinary speed in which the Internet has developed and spread, faster than any other previous medium, and the speed at which society has developed its capacity to adapt to it.
- The endemic fear of the new, accentuated by the panic transmitted by the media (moral panic), labeling the Internet as impossible to regulate and as a source of danger for young people.
- The newness of this medium means that, in many cases, the skills of young people exceed those of their parents and teachers and that they can therefore use the technologies better and evade adult control.

Parallel to the expansion of Internet use among young people, parents' fears have also grown concerning the use that they may make of the Net. According to data from the Eurobarometer of 2008, most European parents were concerned by this problem. Hence, 65 percent were shown to be quite concerned that their children could access images of explicit sex or violence; 60 percent that they could become victims of grooming; 55 percent that they could obtain information that may lead them to self-harm, suicide, or anorexia; 54 percent that they would be bullied by other minors through the Internet (cyberbullying); and 47 percent that they could publish private or personal information on the Internet.

Most authors agree that the Internet is perceived by the minor as a diverse and flexible medium, full of new opportunities. Sonia Livingstone and Magdalena Bober of the London School of Economics, in the conclusions of the UK Children Go Online project, indicate that children and young people see the Internet as "a flexible and diverse medium, helping them to find information for school and homework, communicating with friends from school and relatives using email, instant messaging and chat rooms, as well as playing games, downloading music and visiting fan sites" (2003, 10). "Fun," "communication," and "information" tend to be the words used most often by minors to define what the Internet means for them. However, this perception of the Net is very different from that of their parents.

Parents firmly believe that the Internet's greatest function resides in its usefulness as an educational tool. Not only do they consider it to be a school resource, but they also believe that the information they can find on the Internet may help their children in many ways. Karen E. Soeters and Katinka Van Schaik (2006, 35) argue that, according to parents, the Internet also "helps to establish their likes and dislikes and provides knowledge on sensitive subjects." The data obtained by EU Kids Online also considers the fact that parents see the Internet as an opportunity for accessing information in general, while, on the other hand, they tend not to value the social relations that their children may have on the Internet and the entertainment factor.

Mediation Strategies

Parents' perceptions of the media and the influence it can have on children determine their mediation of the minor's relation with technology. As with other media, parents develop different strategies for mediating children's Internet activities. These strategies include the establishing of rules and restrictions, "social approaches" (to see, share, or talk about children's activities on the Internet), and the use of technological tools to filter or monitor their Internet use. Generally, parents prefer to talk with their children about what they do online and to be close by when they are connected; in the case of smaller children, this is because the parents want to share their experiences with them, and in the case of older children because parents think that rules do not work well at their age.

The way in which regulation policies for the Internet and minors are applied in Europe may explain, to a certain extent, why parents' and children's perceptions about Internet opportunities are so divergent. The public discourse directly affects the ways in which parents act. The basic conception of opportunities relates to Internet activities including entertainment, information, education, communication and socialization on social networks, creativity, and civic participation. According to data gathered by EU Kids Online, this heterogeneous set of activities awakens considerable optimism in terms of both public sector and private sector provisions (Hasebrink et al. 2009).

The National Context

Parents' perceptions are therefore affected by their different national contexts. One of the studies considered as part of the EU Kids Online program was an analysis of the different national contexts in which the perception of the Internet and its risks is based.

The Work of the Press

As indicated earlier, the work of the media is one of the factors that must be taken into account in order to unravel society's picture of the Internet's risks and opportunities. In order to consider the media coverage of the relation between the Internet and minors, EU Kids Online analyzed the press content of fourteen member countries of the research network. In order to cover as wide a spectrum as possible of the press, the research considered three different types of written media in each country: one national and considered-to-be-quality press, another regional, and another of the so-called popular press.

Among the main conclusions of the study, it is worth noting that 70 percent of the pieces mention the risks involved minors' Internet use, in contrast to the 30 percent that mention the opportunities that the Internet offers young people. Among the risks mentioned, and in line with EU Kids Online's classification of risks, those related to violence or sex appeared in 46 percent and 38 percent, respectively, while opportunities related to education amounted to scarcely 9 percent.

Another significant aspect is the subject matter covered by the different pieces analyzed. These subjects were divided into three types: those related to legal, criminal, or police matters; those related to education; and those related to games, entertainment, or free time. In almost all countries, news related to legal, criminal, and police matters was present in half or more of the pieces analyzed. In the cases of Austria, Portugal, and Greece, they were present in 68 percent, 64 percent, and 61 percent, respectively. In contrast, it is noteworthy that subjects related to education and entertainment (the two aspects most clearly defined as opportunities) hardly find their way into the news. Except for the case of Austria and Estonia, in which education is present in at least half of the news analyzed, in the other countries, it has a presence of between 10 and 25 percent. A case apart is that of Denmark, which does not follow the general tendency and where entertainment and games are present in 81 percent of the news while those related to legal, criminal, and police matters hardly reaches 14 percent.

Table 5.2. Percentage of Stories in the Three Main Story Types

Country	Legal, crime, and police stories	Education	Entertainment, play, and leisure stories	Total number of stories
Austria	68%	57%	19%	72
Belgium	59%	14%	22%	79
Denmark	14%	14%	81%	21
Estonia	56%	53%	30%	116
Germany	40%	26%	21%	122
Greece	61%	11%	23%	44
Ireland	44%	26%	34%	50
Italy	56%	12%	18%	90
Norway	40%	15%	20%	104
Portugal	64%	7%	7%	56
Slovenia	57%	15%	30%	80
Spain	61%	12%	12%	130
United Kingdom	49%	17%	13%	63

Source: Haddon and Stald (2008).

Parents' Use of the Internet

The Eurobarometer of 2008 also shows the importance of cultural differences. The lower levels of concern and mediation among Nordic parents, despite their greater use of the Internet, may be due to the more permissive Internet policies applied to young people or even to a greater level of confidence in young people themselves. The Eurobarometer suggests that if parents are Internet users, they carry out better or more mediation of their children's use of the Internet, whereas those who do not use the Internet mediate less.

The concerns that parents have regarding their children's Internet use are reflected in the mediation strategies applied to minors, many of which have consequences for the child's development. Thus, it can be seen that usage restrictions occupy an important part of the job of mediation, and in many cases, limitations in usage may also mean a significant limitation of the child's freedom of expression.

These concerns vary depending on the different countries and, to a large extent, on Internet penetration. In fact, the relation between the level of parental concern and the percentage of minors who use the Internet is negative. In other words, countries in which minors use less Internet are the ones in which parents are most worried, while in countries with a greater level of penetration among minors, such as Sweden or Denmark, the level of concern is lower.

Similarly, the use that parents make of the Internet also affects their perceptions of the risks for minors. Likewise, a lower Internet usage among parents results in a higher level of concern about the risk of the Internet for minors.

Conclusions

The aspects highlighted in this chapter, such as the positioning of the media or the specific national contexts of Internet usage, as well as the technological abilities of parents, are important factors in terms of the influence they have on parents' job of mediation, crucial to ensuring minors' correct use of the Internet. According to Eurobarometer data, most European parents prefer the "social mediation" strategy to "restrictive mediation." In this sense, an excessive level of alarm about the consequences and influences of Internet use may lead parents into more restrictive practices and, in a way that is rarely constructive, may keep minors away from the Internet or negatively influence their use of it.

Although the disparity in national contexts makes it difficult to establish a general line on the influence of these factors, tendencies in terms of these aspects' influence can be established that lead us to conclude that parents' greater use and knowledge of the Internet results in less anxiety with regards to minors' use of it. In the same way, Internet penetration may be relevant in countries where penetration has been very sudden, such as Eastern European countries, where there has been an even greater gap between parents' Internet skills and those of their children, which has resulted in a greater level of parental concern. These phenomena, however, represent temporary problems in the face of the gradual generalization of Internet use.

From the data presented here, it can be concluded that even though much has been done (and must continue to be done) to raise awareness of Internet risks, hardly anything has been done to explain the changes in young people's social relations that this usage involves, which is essential to understand the use that minors make of communication technologies. Peer relations among minors are also different with contact between them now being permanent. For many young people, something cannot be thought of as fun or entertaining if it is not enjoyed through the Internet. If the opinions of the minors themselves and the satisfaction they gain from these new communication forms are not taken into account, then they will be deprived of correctly using the opportunities that the Net offers (Regan, Porter, and Sanchez 2005, 503; Livingstone and Bober 2003; Byron 2008).

Normally, regulatory policies focus on content, often based on moral panic, that is harmful for minors, while leaving out of the public debate the genuine reasons why young people use these new technologies and how this use contributes toward the establishment of new ties within the family itself (Regan, Porter, and Sanchez 2005, 504).

The still-widespread ignorance of what different Internet uses can really mean for young people has resulted in researchers being divided into two clear tendencies: those who try to see the benefits that using the Internet has for minors and those who only analyze the risks arising from this use. Most of the studies analyzed and the literature reviewed indicate that positive experiences, or the benefits that minors obtain from Internet use, are rarely the object of study and that, instead, the risks involved always become the studies' key focus. On too many occasions, this pessimistic vision, influenced by what the English-speaking world calls moral panic, means that the child's status as an active citizen participating in society is rejected.

References

AccesoMetrix. 2003. *Estudio sobre la cobertura mediática y tono informativo del medio Internet.* Accessed January 17, 2012. www.acceso.com/internet/estudio1.html.

Byron, Tanya. 2008. *Safer Children in a Digital World: The Report of the Byron Review.* London: Department for Children, Schools and Families, and the Department for Culture, Media and Sport.

Castells, Manuel. 2010. *The Information Age: Economy, Society, and Culture.* Vol. 1, *The Rise of Network Society.* 2nd ed. Oxford, UK: Blackwell Publishers.

Haddon, Leslie, and Gitte Stald. 2008. "A Comparative Analysis of European Media Coverage of Children and the Internet." Paper presented at the Association of Internet Researchers Conference, IT University, Copenhagen, October 16–19.

Hasebrink, Uwe, Sonia Livingstone, Leslie Haddon, Lucinda Kirwil, and Cristina Ponte. 2007. *Comparing Children's Online Activities and Risks across Europe: A Preliminary Report Comparing Findings for Poland, Portugal and UK: A Report for the EC Safer Internet Plus Programme.* Accessed January 17, 2012. www.cyberethics.info/cyethics2/UserFiles/EUKidsOnline_ComparisonChildrensOnlineActiviti es&Risks_PolandPortugalUk_2007.pdf.

Littlewood, Anne. 2003. "Cyberporn and Moral Panic: An Evaluation of Press Reactions to Pornography on the Internet." *Library and Information Research* 27, no. 86 (Summer): 8–18.

Livingstone, Sonia, and Magdalena Bober. 2003. *UK Children Go Online: Listening to Young People's Experiences.* London: London School of Economics and Political Science.

Livingstone, Sonia, and Leslie Haddon, eds. 2009. *Kids Online: Opportunities and Risks for Children.* Bristol, UK: Polity Press.

Livingstone, Sonia, and Ellen J. Helsper. 2006. "Does Advertising Literacy Mediate the Effects of Advertising on Children? A Critical Examination of Two Linked Research Literatures in Relation to Obesity and Food Choice." *Journal of Communication* 56, no. 3: 560–84.

———. 2007. "Gradations in Digital Inclusion: Children, Young People and the Digital Divide." *New Media and Society* 9, no. 4: 671–96.

Regan, Leslie, Nikki Porter, and Wendy Sanchez. 2005. "You Can See Anything on the Internet, You Can Do Anything on the Internet! Young Canadians Talk about the Internet." *Canadian Journal of Communication* 30: 503–26.

Riddell, Jamie. 1995. "Pornography on the Internet: A New Moral Panic?" B.A. diss., Queen Margaret University College, Edinburgh.

Rössler, Patrick. 2001. "Between Online Heaven and Cyberhell: The Framing of 'the Internet' by Traditional Media Coverage in Germany." *New Media & Society* 3, no. 1: 49–66.

Sandywell, Barry. 2006. "Monsters in Cyberspace: Cyberphobia and Cultural Panic in the Information Age." *Information, Communication and Society* 9, no. 1: 39–61.

Soeters, Karen E., and Katinka Van Schaik. 2006. "Children's Experiences on the Internet." *New Library World* 107, nos. 1–2: 31–36.

6

The Psychosocial Recovery Processes in Victims of Violence and Terrorist Acts

Juan de Dios Uriarte

Translated by Julie Waddington

After fifty years of politically motivated acts of violence in Spain, particularly in the Basque Country, one of the most widespread conclusions drawn is that the social impact and damages caused by them have been enormous. Terrorism has changed the lives, feelings, and relationships of many people, turning them into victims of a conflict that they did not feel part of.

A shared definition of the term *terrorism* has still not been found because of the different cultural, political, and historical frameworks of those who promote it on the one hand and are affected by it on the other. An analysis of 109 definitions carried out by Alex P. Schmidt and Albert I. Jongman (1988; five in Lima 2006, 46) concludes that the term refers to intentional, persistent, and unpredictable acts of violence and to the use of force to bring about changes in the ideas and behavior of others or to achieve political, social, and economic objectives. It is also a resource used by criminal organizations to challenge the state and the institutions that try to stop them and prevent them from committing crime, as in the case of narcotrafficking.

We can provisionally understand that a victim is any person who suffers emotional distress of variable intensity as a result of deliberate physical, social, or economic damage caused by another human being

(Echeburúa 2007). This definition includes those affected physically and emotionally while carrying out emergency rescue tasks with victims of terrorist acts.

The specific nature of terrorist violence means that it is highly more likely to cause social and psychological upheaval than mass accidents or natural disasters, and its consequences are more difficult to cope with, even with professional help. This can be explained by some of its specific characteristics (Nemeroff et al. 2006; Cabrera, Martín Beristain, Jiménez, and Páez 2006, 110): it is not accidental but avoidable; the subjects have no way of preventing it, protecting themselves, or preparing themselves psychologically; and no intelligible justification or understanding can be found between ends and means. More pain is experienced when it is perceived that the perpetrator has acted with outright vengeance, indifferent to the suffering of others, intending to cause as much damage as possible, and not caring if there are other casualties who are even more innocent, such as children, old people, or people with disabilities. Enrique Echeburúa (2004) suggests that a terrorist attack produces in victims a feeling of injustice and powerlessness, the loss of basic confidence and integrity of the self, mistrust in institutions, and despair concerning the human being.

In general, terrorist acts do not have explicit objectives except to make their presence known and to terrorize society, to produce insecurity or generalized suffering (Fullerton et al. 2003), so that the terrorist actions transcend the victims in order to reach the public in a way that would not be possible by any other means. In this sense, the whole of society becomes a collective victim when it feels threatened and therefore modifies certain kinds of social behavior; mistrust and fear of public expression are generated, legitimate political aspirations and necessary police and judicial actions are surrendered, with the belief that by acting this way, terrorist threats will not turn into attacks causing more victims.

Currently, resilience is a subject of positive psychology that highlights the capacity for coping, for recovery, and even for the positive transformation and improvement of the person who has suffered any kind of trauma (Grotberg 2002). Applied to the sphere of victimization, it cannot be affirmed a priori that those affected by collective acts of violence will develop psychosocial pathologies. There is evidence to show that most people affected by traumas, including those of a terrorist nature, are capable of moving on positively and finding peace in themselves and with their surroundings, despite the inevitable problems and difficulties involved.

In terms of the community, the question of resilience relates to the community's capacity to respond to environmental disasters, armed conflicts, terrorism, and other problems. The range of fields of application has expanded the meaning of resilience, often making it less precise and sometimes resulting in it being used metaphorically (Francart 2010).

The Psychological Consequences of Terrorism

According to data provided by the Colectivo de Víctimas del Terrorismo del País Vasco (Victims of Terrorism of the Basque Country), 1,299 people have died in Spain as a result of terrorist acts: 953 caused by the organization ETA, 201 by another group supporting Islamic ideology, 34 by right-wing groups, 83 by the extreme left-wing group Grupo de Resistencia Antifascista Primero de Octubre, and 28 as a result of the acts of the so-called Grupos Antiterroristas de Liberación. By contrast, the Ministry of the Interior of the Spanish government recognizes 9,522 victims of terrorism, of which 1,382 have been killed (*El País*, March 6, 2010). The report drawn up by Ararteko—the Ombudsman's Office of the Basque Country for the Institutional Care of Victims of Terrorism in Euskadi—reveals that 16,000 people have been injured by ETA terrorist acts, 70 have been kidnapped, thousands have fled the Basque Country as a result of the terrorism, and 42,000 are potential targets by belonging to one of the threatened groups. In the study published in 2005 by the Centre for Sociological Research, 70 percent of Spanish people believed that all citizens were victims of terrorism and more than 30 percent admitted to feeling "personally affected" by terrorism (Llera and Retortillo 2005).

Different types of victims have been established with regards to different aspects of terrorism. Direct victims are those who have suffered damages, of a physical, economic, or psychological nature. Both direct victims, and those affected by the death of a first-degree relative as a result of a terrorist attack, are known as primary victims. Indirect and secondary victims are those who belong to the direct victim's family and close social network and have strong emotional ties with them; their relationships are affected by the events, and they can sometimes suffer from posttraumatic stress. There are also those referred to as peripheral victims, who, from afar or through the media, identify with the direct victims, with a significant connection being visible between the violent events and their impact (Maeseele et al. 2008). There are those at risk of becoming victims who, because of personal or contextual circumstances, become an "easier" or more "accessible" target than others, due to their living conditions, lack of self-protection measures, links to other direct targets, and so on; on the other hand there are vulnerable victims whose lives and circumstances may mean that they are even more affected by terrorist acts than others with greater coping capacities (Echeburúa, Corral, and Amor 2002; Echeburúa 2004; Larizgoitia, Izarzugaza, and Markez 2009). There are unknown or silent victims who, because they do not exteriorize their distress, are not included in the records and do not receive any health-care services.

Terrorist acts are stressful, serious, and acute events or situations that affect many people at the same time, albeit in varying degrees depending on their nature and on the victim's relation to the events, or with those directly involved in them. In general, they involve real danger to life or a threat to physical and psychological integrity, affecting well-being and personal and social needs, but it is extremely difficult to predict what the consequences may be in the people who are exposed to situations that can be so different in nature (Larizgoitia, Izarzugaza, and Markez 2009): being a spectator is very different from being a direct victim in the same way that enduring material losses is quite different from losing loved ones; being affected individually or as the member of a collective group; being the victim of a one-off attack or of continuous acts; or being the victim of an attack, kidnapping, extortion, or persecution (Echeburúa 2004). It is also important to consider the psychological nature of the person, the social support he or she has, and the cultural significance of the act, as these are aspects that will determine the way in which the psychological damages caused by terrorism will take their course (Cyrulnik 2005).

Terrorist acts produce imbalance and emotional distress that is reflected in different psychical and psychological symptoms. In the first moments, a shock is produced that makes it difficult to think or feel normally; there is a feeling of unreality and loss of control over one's life. After that come into play fear, anger, distrust of one's surroundings and institutions, a continuous feeling of being on the alert, depression, crying, and loneliness. After the initial moments, other symptoms often appear: a lowering of self-esteem and self-confidence, the loss of vital interests, feelings of depersonalization, an increase in vulnerability, problems sleeping, sexual dysfunctions, changes in one's system of social and other values (Echeburúa, Corral, and Amor 2002; Larizgoitia, Izarzugaza, and Markez 2009).

Until now, no conclusive results have been obtained from research on the psychological damage caused to victims of terrorism in the Basque

Country. Enrique Echeburúa, Paz de Corral, and Pedro Javier Amor (2002, 143) suggest that the prevalence of posttraumatic stress in victims of terrorism is high (66.7 percent of the sample), significantly higher than in victims of domestic violence and similar in terms of percentages if compared to victims of sexual violence (69.9 percent of those assessed). Other factors that have an impact on the damages caused are the type of victim and the psychical consequences that the survivors may suffer from (Echeburúa 2004).

Itziar Larizgoitia, Isabel Izarzugaza, and Iñaki Markez (2009) compare the damages suffered by victims of terrorism with a sample of the general population who claimed not to have suffered from violence and another group who had suffered some kind of violence. Primary victims of terrorism have between three and four times more health problems that lead to disabilities and require continuous medical treatment; 43 percent present higher instances of psychiatric symptoms that carry a greater risk of becoming psychiatric cases than in the other groups: their physical and emotional distress is between four and seven times higher than in the general population, almost triple the level in the group of victims of other types of violence; and the feeling of solitude and perceived social stigmatization is between 1.5 and 1.7 greater than in the other groups.

Through a survey carried out with 750 victims of terrorism, Enrique Baca and María Luisa Cabanas (1997) concluded that victims were around 2.5 times more at risk of suffering mental health problems than the rest of the population, and that they experienced poorer quality of life, poorer psychological well-being, and a higher incidence of being overburdened at work. Direct victims presented different levels of anxiety, depression, and psychosomatic problems and higher levels of social dysfunction than indirect victims. A later study carried out among victims of terrorism in the Basque Country found that 55 percent of direct victims and 45 percent of the people threatened are likely to suffer from mental health problems. The prevalence of problems associated with depression is around 68 percent and 80 percent, anxiety problems between 50 percent and 63 percent, and social phobia between 41 percent and 50 percent (Conejero 2009).

Researchers have found different factors that impact psychological damages: the physical proximity to the place of the attack (Cano et al. 2004; Fullerton et al. 2003; Ganzel et al. 2007); familiarity with and emotional closeness to the direct victim (Conejero 2009, 113); the highly stressful personal experiences gone through, whether these are of a terrorist nature or any other type; and the social habituation to the possibility of terrorist attacks (Bleich et al. 2006).

For both research and clinical purposes, and in terms of any psychosocial intervention, it is important to differentiate between symptoms of stress related to a traumatic event and to stress disorder itself. Beyond the reactive symptomatology of the first moments, the concept of psychological problems takes in persistent behavioral, emotional, cognitive, and social changes that significantly limit the person's ability to take control of his or her life. After 11-M in Madrid, the results relating to the probability of posttraumatic stress disorder varied from 1.9 percent to 13.3 percent of the population, depending on the instruments and criteria of evaluation. Carmelo Vázquez, Pau Pérez-Sales, and Georg Matt (2006) conclude that these results show the importance of establishing a precise definition of posttraumatic stress.

The disorder that affects victims of terrorism has at least three basic components: (1) the physical, psychological, and social damage; (2) the representation of the facts in terms of the victim, incomprehension, punishment, being forgotten, or solidarity, which is conditioned by social and political considerations; and (3) the resentment and fear that keeps them alert in the face of potential future damages. Clinical psychology tends to understand psychological problems at an intrapsychic and individual level, assessing the 1 and 3 type components, but not taking into account component 2, the sociocultural and intergroup dimension within which the terrorist phenomena is inscribed. The social context of many terrorist acts carried out in the Basque Country has involved the support, exaltation, and public recognition of the perpetrators; the social stigmatization of the victims; and the silence, incomprehension, and sometimes continuous persecution of those very victims and their families (Cabrera et al. 2006). In this sense, the real traumas of terrorism are psychosocial ones (Blanco and Díaz 2004) that are difficult to overcome if professional help is not provided and if this is not accompanied by a discourse that supports and dignifies the victims.

Not everything is negative. There also appear to be some positive effects noted by the victims themselves: they perceive more of a bond and more trust between themselves and their affective environment, and they experience a renewal of the energy to fight, to move on, with new relations, new hopes, and new feelings; in short, they discover values and previously unknown qualities for coping positively (Larizgoitia, Izarzugaza, and Markez 2009).

Individual Resilience and Terrorism

Different explanations exist as to why many people who have suffered situations of mistreatment, abandonment, abuse, exploitation, and misery have been able to subsequently move on and carry out a normal life. One of these is based on the idea that, usually, most people are not entirely happy or totally unhappy. Consequently, after the traumatic experiences, the positive emotions of the victims do not disappear completely but rather coexist with the negative and stressful ones, helping to reduce anxiety and to enable the victim to recuperate (Vera 2004). The question of resilience is presented on similar lines. The process whereby those affected by a severe traumatic experience are able to overcome adversity and return to their previous level of psychological well-being is referred to as resilience. Whether understood as a process or as a result, researchers have high-lighted a series of competences, skills, and personal qualities and social resources that tend to be present in resilient people.

Different studies carried out after mass traumatic events such as those of September 11, 2001, in the United States; March 11, 2004, in Madrid; and July 7, 2005, in London confirm that many of those involved (40–78.2 percent) presented either none or, if any, very minor psychological aftereffects (Bleich et al. 2006; Hobfoll et al. 2009). Many presented moderate symptoms of stress and adaptive dysfunction, but the symptoms diminished or disappeared after six to twelve months (Vera, Carbelo, and Vecina 2006). Resilience was the most common reason, and the traumatic symptoms were less intense than initially expected (Vázquez 2005).

Trajectories of Resilience in Cases of Terrorism

The way in which victims deal with experiences of collective violence does not follow a common behavioral pattern. Many studies on terrorism have focused on the vulnerability of the victim and on the psychological damage caused: the posttraumatic stress, the anxiety and depression, among other aspects. By contrast, relatively few studies have focused on people's capacity for resilience when data exist indicating that many of those affected and involved in terrorist attacks do not present posttraumatic symptoms and that others recover from the hardships suffered in a short period of time (Vázquez 2005; Vera 2004).

Terrorist acts produce situations that are so exceptional and that threaten personal integrity in such a way that the expected responses are equally exceptional or different from those usually manifested in the face of less dangerous situations. Based on this premise, and from a psycho-pathological viewpoint, at least two basic trajectories can be considered in terms of the affected people's response: the reactive trajectory and the structural trajectory.

The reactive trajectory is characterized by a series of emotional, psychological, and physical changes that tend to manifest themselves in victims after the violent occurrence: fear, anger, sadness, desperation, dis-ordered thinking, disorientation, sleeping and eating disorders, avoidance behavior, isolation, intrusive thoughts, and so on. These symptoms tend to diminish with the passage of time when the threats abate and the emotions associated with the memory of the event subside, and as the subject recuperates their family, working, and social normality.

The structural trajectory characterizes those cases in which the initial symptomatology is the same as in the previous model but does not diminish over time and hinders personal adaptation, subjective well-being, and social relations—meaning that the victim does not recover the level of functioning they had before the crisis, despite all attempts. Whether on the basis of objective indicators or not, subjects still feel under threat and that the risk of attack is imminent, their emotional state is high, and their state of alert remains intense and inappropriate to the reality of the situation (Bonanno 2004). These kinds of victims need professional help to overcome trauma. Moreover, some cases that start without initial symptomatology but that subsequently present symptoms of delayed stress can be included in this model (Vera 2004). In both cases, the cognitive variables and personality traits of the victims are determining factors, as well as their way of processing information and emotions. Knowing what the "normal" and proportionate responses to a traumatic experience are, and which are "abnormal," disproportionate, and inefficient, would represent a starting point in terms of a coping strategy.

In view of this psychopathological model, the salutogenic or resilience model considers three trajectories for the victims of terrorism: stability trajectory, recuperation trajectory, and transformation trajectory.

The stability trajectory understands resilience as resistance and immunity: faced with the terrorist attack, the subject is able to remain psychically intact and to withstand the difficulties arising from it without symptoms of stress; the subject is able to move on without psychological changes in a risk environment, even with more or less continuous threats or persecution.

The recuperation trajectory is the ability to return to the previous state, to have a meaningful and normal life after having suffered significant psychological damage. Victims are able to regain control over their lives and over their emotional responses, to put the trauma behind them while not remaining a prisoner to terrorism's memory (Cyrulnik 2005). The temporal dimension is taken into account here, as regards the disappearance of the initial symptoms: people or a group will be more resilient the sooner they are able to recuperate. The resilience approach suggests that there are elements of resilience in all people that, either by themselves or with the help of resilience tutors, can return to normality after being affected by violent and traumatic events.

The transformation trajectory involves a more complex dimension of resilience according to which in some cases people are capable of withstanding the experience, and in other cases are able to recover and even make positive changes in the sense of attaining higher levels of confidence in their own abilities and greater self-esteem. The experience has mobilized their resources, values, and personal relations, and their lives have acquired new meaning and opportunities. This posttraumatic personal growth is consistent with times of negative emotions and with stressful experiences (Calhoun and Tedeschi 1999). This approach emphasizes human plasticity, creativity, and the biophilic and positive orientation of the human being (Hobfoll et al. 2009).

Resilience Factors in Victims of Terrorism

Many of the possibilities for resilience emerge from the discourse that victims construct from the events, which are at the same time influenced by the social discourse they take on board from their surroundings (Maeseele et al. 2008). The resilient discourse, as opposed to embarrassment and concealment, highlights the pride of the direct and indirect victims, their personal dignity; it is aimed at understanding, explaining, and trying to find some meaning out of what happened, even though the conclusion may be drawn that no meaning can be found in the senselessness of it. It is not about refusing to remember or feel—although it is a good idea to try to reduce the emotions associated with past events and their consequences—but rather about avoiding revictimization and the constant expression of the affliction in an attempt to seek attention, compassion, or overprotection. It is a discourse, in short, that reflects the conviction that life deserves to be lived despite what has happened, and one that maintains confidence in others.

The proactive attitudes that show subjects feeling in control of their own life and asking, "What can I do now so as not suffer any more?" also demonstrates their resilience. Here we can include the self-defense mechanisms that help to keep emotions under a certain amount of control: attitudes of opposition to and active avoidance of the memories and feelings of unhappiness, depression, fear, and solitude that come over them; attempts to minimize the events by comparing them to other known or possible situations—not in order to diminish their relevance but as a strategy to reduce the associated emotions; the active seeking of well-being and happiness, and living every moment of life with intensity and with loved ones; and highlighting optimism and positive thinking, without falling into a false euphoria, have all had a healing effect for victims.

Affective and social bonds are strong resources of resilience. In one's relations with others, one can air the problem, share one's feelings, and therefore seek relief from distress (Rimé, Páez, and Martínez 2004). The feelings of family members and friends and the way they face the situation will affect the victim's development and help in a way that may be more effective than that of mental health professionals. If the family and social relations are a source of stress, sometimes isolation is an option as valid as that of professional help.

Some people help themselves by helping others. Victims may be extremely brave on behalf of other victims by telling them that they are not alone, that their reactions and feelings are understandable (Larizgoitia, Izarzugaza, and Markez 2009; Martín and Paéz 2000). Concern for others and disinterested help are resilience factors. On the other hand, participating in self-help groups may be a more significant means of emotional support, even more so than the support of family and other forms of social support (Durá and Hernández 2003). Self-help groups can have therapeutic benefits if they overcome the tendency toward revictimization and are guided by professionals.

Community Resilience in the Face of Terrorism

The persistence of a terrorist organization such as ETA, which has been active in the Basque Country since 1959, cannot be explained without taking into account its origins and the political and social framework that it feeds on, justifies itself on, and at times is driven by. In order to demonstrate how ETA's violent acts are justified by some population sectors, the 2009 report drawn up by Ararteko, the Ombudsman Institution of the

Basque Parliament, indicates that 14.8 percent of young people between twelve and sixteen years old are not against ETA, and another 14 percent are in intermediate positions of rejection or are indifferent to the subject (Ararteko: Defensoría del Pueblo 2009, 383–84). In addition, the Sociological Studies Office of the Basque Government, in collaboration with the Basque Youth Observatory, after an opinion poll with young Basque people between fifteen and twenty-nine years old, reveals worrying data: only six out of ten people questioned outrightly rejected terrorism; a similar percentage, higher than 50 percent, would not like to have a member of ETA (55 percent) or a person threatened by the terrorist group (51 percent) as a neighbor (*El Correo*, February 26, 2010).

The community dimension of resilience relates to the capacity of the social system and institutions to carry out significant and deliberate actions to prevent and deal collectively with the conflicts facing them and to subsequently reorganize themselves to improve the way they work, their structures, and their identity (Pfefferbaum et al. 2007; Suárez-Ojeda, Fara, and Márquez 2007; Walsh 2007). This relates more to the tangible and intangible resources and capacities inherent in the community, which are mobilized in the face of disasters, than to the external resources that may be made available (Maguire and Cartwright 2008).

For terrorists, victims are not important as people. Terrorists' objectives are to violate reality, intimidate, cause a commotion, and create insecurity in the general population in order to achieve the largest audience for their political goals and to take revenge on an impersonal enemy. In this sense, community resilience refers to society's ability to deal with the attack; to tend to victims; to facilitate group recovery with initiatives that help prevent intimidation, persecution, and extortion; and to definitively eradicate future terrorist attacks, actively and firmly expressing social repudiation of violence and maintaining organization and control over social life, despite the violent attempts to alter it (Twigg 2007). This includes the community's ability to carry on normally, paying no attention to terrorists' interests, not even by omission.

Community resilience must identify and tend to groups and individuals under threat and at a higher risk of attack with protective and self-protective measures, not treating them as separate from the rest of the community but rather including them and prioritizing the elimination of risks and the safety of the group before that of individuals (Walsh 2007). The need for social protection, the attention to crisis situations produced by attacks, and the elimination of terrorism cannot be achieved solely through improvements in information systems, or with the increase, training, and coordination of professional resources in policing skills. The involvement of the whole community is needed. The way in which these measures are managed by political representatives and the authorities will determine the community's ability to overcome possible damages (Fullerton et al. 2003).

In recent history, examples can be found of collective responses to kidnaps and terrorist attacks, of solidarity with victims of terrorism, of spontaneous and selfless responses to emergency situations and catastrophes, and of aid being given to communities and victims of other sociopolitical conflicts. When these situations occur, the most positive qualities emerge in many people, including those they were unaware they had, and they are quick to join in the reconstruction of the city and its services, to act on behalf of the collective good. Some of these experiences remain in society's collective memory and boost its self-esteem (Uriarte 2010).

The first reactions to indiscriminate terrorist attacks with massive damages are not necessarily negative or unhealthy and do not necessarily produce "social chaos" (San Juan 2001, 22). For example, the people of London who lived through the attacks of July 7, 2005, and were aware of the threats hanging over airlines, decided to continue using public transport (Verleye et al. 2008; Lima 2006). There are also frequent cases of positive coping behavior, of helping the emergency services, and of mutual aid, even when there are no predetermined guidelines for this or when these are insufficient. People also behave in an organized way after the initial commotion, helping those at their side despite their own pain; emotional crises do not predominate, and fear and anger do not necessarily lead to desperation and flight if these are not necessary. The instructions of an authority or a person who assumes the lead are soon heeded. Looting, robberies, and assaults are not frequent, even though these tend to be highlighted on television, and are often related to social and ethnic conflicts or issues related to deprivation that were already pronounced before the crisis (Páez, Fernández, and Martín 2001). A minority is affected by so-called posttraumatic stress while the majority of victims reveals a sufficient ability to absorb the shock, which is not perceived as a reason for seeking psychological help (Pfefferbaum et al. 2007). The initial disorientation and vulnerability are immediately counterposed by behavior showing sympathy to the victims and their families and of self-affirmation as a compensation mechanism: the exaltation of one's own values, an increase in political involvement, demonstrations, widespread mourning, spontaneous placing of flowers and photographs, acts of homage to and remembrance of the victims.

The Pillars of Community Resilience

Experts in disaster situations and terrorism highlight the characteristics and types of behavior that define a resilient community. Generally speaking, the more resilient societies tend to be those in which there is less inequality (economic, cultural, social), in which social cohesion prevails in the face of conflict, and in which there are measures in place for integration and social participation, with legitimate and honest representatives. Furthermore, cultural identity helps to reinforce the solidarity links in cases of social emergency and provides a response to the damages produced to cultural heritage and the environment. Humanitarian and solidarity acts, whether for one's fellow citizens or in terms of aid from outside the community, also form the basis for resilience in the face of exceptional situations (Pfefferbaum et al. 2007; Suárez-Ojeda, Fara, and Márquez 2007).

Society must feel that government officials and security forces are strongly determined and dispose of any means necessary to detain the perpetrators and those who support them, back them, or collaborate with them indirectly. With an honest government, the appropriate authority and justice system, society as a whole, individuals, institutions, associations, services, and businesses will be more eager to cooperate voluntarily and will even be more willing to accept potentially "negative" results.

Citizens' rights to information require the correct treatment of communications related to terrorism. Honest information changes attitudes, preferences, perceived risks, and behavior; ambiguous information creates doubts and speculation of the measures themselves; partial information, or biased information toward one side, leads to rejection. It is therefore important to appropriately inform with regards to the content, frequency, and scope of information, but without creating unnecessary social alarm or presenting the most negative frightening scenarios that unnecessarily elevate the "terror tax" (Maeseele et al. 2008, 62). When populations are accustomed to being kept adequately informed by the authorities, confidence in these authorities is strengthened; personal worries, pessimism, and the perception of the risk of attack are reduced; and preventative and remedial action is dealt with better and more promptly (Acinas 2007; Francart 2010). In antiterrorist politics, people appreciate good governmental communication over and above other kinds of initiatives (Maseele et al. 2008).

Support for victims of terrorism must be the primary goal of anti-terrorist initiatives of the community. This includes both the ideological, social, and institutional delegitimization of violence and its perpetrators in all spheres: public, school, family, and so on, as well as the norms, principles, and acts that recognize the victims' dignity and aims to heal the damages suffered. This is expressed through shared feelings, by letting them know that they are not alone, showing empathy and solidarity, and demonstrating that society as a whole has been attacked through the victim and that the victim's psychological and moral recovery is inseparable from that of the rest of the population; through the support of all that normalizes their everyday lives without them having to leave their home, without giving up power or public spaces to the perpetrators and those who support them, expressing ideas freely and expressly supporting those who stand up to them and condemn their threats and extortion.

These beliefs confirm one of the most important pillars of community resilience, by defining the meaning of existence and specifically the patterns of social interaction and behavior in the face of terrorism. There are approaches in favor of community resilience that try to understand the events and evaluate them in a way that reinforces society's conviction that its forces will overcome difficulties and win the fight against terrorism (Bleich et al. 2006).

These represent resilient approaches, a biophilic and positive conception of man and society, that aspire to the universalization of human rights and social justice, and that are opposed to fundamentalisms that generate radicality, intolerance, lack of solidarity, and pessimism toward life. Attitudes in favor of a nonviolent culture at all interpersonal relationship levels must be encouraged from infancy, in the family, school, and media.

Although surprising at first sight, social humor has been considered as a strategy of resilience. This refers to some people's ability to "find the comic in the tragic," which helps to lighten or remove the bitterness from certain difficult situations, to remove oneself emotionally, and to be able to analyze the situation more objectively. The ability to laugh together about certain social, political, or religious stereotypes applied to oneself or to others reinforces the feeling of belonging and makes the community more resilient (Carbelo and Jáuregui 2006).

The Possibility of Forgiveness

Forgiveness is a resilient resource in interpersonal conflicts and has an important place in the psychological overcoming of the effects of terrorist violence. Forgiveness, together with the reconciliation, reparation, and disconnection that have been present in other social and political conflicts (Northern Ireland, South Africa, Chile, Argentina, Guatemala, El Salvador), has also made an appearance in Basque Country's political context. Some political leaders, civil organizations, and media representatives are introducing these concepts at a time of the more or less permanent cessation of armed action.

The concepts of reconciliation and forgiveness have different meanings. As Nobel Peace Prize winner Adolfo Pérez Esquivel (2000) indicates, it is important to clarify what is meant by these terms in each individual case, but in any event they are never the same, nor necessarily interdependent, nor in fact essential to achieve political coexistence in the Basque Country. Reconciliation, for example, would mean the previous existence of an interpersonal or intergroup conflict in which the parties, who would have a clearly differentiated cultural and social identity, previously had significant relations and had subsequently been in conflict with each other but now seek mutual understanding, communication, and harmonious coexistence based on the recognition of damages suffered by both parties. This is not, however, a vision of the sociopolitical reality of the Basque Country and of ETA's form of terrorism, which is shared by the majority of the population. Recently, some prisoners guilty of terrorist crimes and in the process of disassociating themselves from ETA have argued that in the future the victims should be asked for forgiveness, and damages caused should be repaired. From the victims' side, however, no reconciliation whatsoever is demanded, but, rather, what they do claim is recognition, justice, and truth. In the Basque Country today, as Susana Conejero (2009, 144) argues, "the question of forgiveness is not considered to be one needing an answer." Not even the victims are demanding that the terrorists ask for forgiveness. But justice does not automatically eliminate resentment, nor does it repair psychological damage.

Associated to a large extent with restorative rather than retributive justice (Strelan, Feather, and Mckee 2008), the terrorists' initiative of saying sorry or asking for forgiveness from the victims implies a recognition of the damage caused and carries with it a positive attitude toward reparation. But granting forgiveness is a decision that belongs solely to the victim; it cannot be replaced by another person or institution and cannot in any circumstances be demanded by the aggressor. As expressed in a newspaper article by Adriana Faranda, who was a member of the Red Brigades: "To ask the victims for forgiveness would be another act of violence: to give them the dilemma of whether to forgive or not would be to add pain to pain" (*El País*, November 26, 2006). Consequently, rather than asking for the forgiveness that may offend victims, it would be best for victims and perpetrators to agree upon acts of remembrance and recognition of the victims, thus sharing the suffering (Conejero 2009).

To pardon the terrorists is not to undermine the legitimacy of the way the victim feels or to suggest this is incorrect or needs correcting, but rather is a possible rational and discretional measure that enables victims to free themselves from resentment, anger, hate, and desire for revenge, insofar as these feelings are internal stressors that they carry around with them and that cause them suffering and psychosomatic damage (Horwitz 2005). In the field of mental health, the disposition to forgiveness may help some victims recover psychological well-being and satisfactory interpersonal relations, to improve their physical and mental functioning, to improve their self-esteem, and to reduce the risk of depression (Conejero 2009; López, Kasanzew, and Fernández 2008).

Forgiveness does not weaken the victim, nor should it be understood as something that may strengthen the perpetrator. To forgive is not to justify what has happened nor to forget it, nor to renounce justice, as it can in fact lead to a greater feeling of justice in victims (Wenzel and Okimoto 2010). Neither does it emerge from a feeling of empathy toward the aggressor, but it is instead an intrapsychic process through which the victim tries to overcome recurrent negative feelings without the need to transform them into positive affects, at the same that they are able to maintain the same negative opinions about what happened (Wade, Bailey, and Shaffer 2005). The aim is that the emotions associated with past traumatic events do not continuously erupt into consciousness, which is not the same as forgetting. Both forgiveness and forgetting are independent psychological resources that the victim can use to overcome the distress that generates hate, and to feel better. From this perspective, the different attitudes expressed on the subject are understandable and acceptable: "I cannot forget nor forgive" (Enrique Múgica, brother of Fernando Múgica, killed by ETA), "I cannot forget but I can forgive" (Lee Ielpi, president of the September 11th Families' Association).

Although traditionally, studies on forgiveness have been linked to theology and justice, in recent decades various empirical studies have been carried out in psychology (for a general overview, see López, Kasanzew, and Fernández 2008), highlighting that fact that the emotions involved in forgiveness whether clemency, anger, remorse, pity, or empathy, may not coincide or have the same relevance in the processes of interpersonal forgiveness as forgiveness in social and political conflicts. From the victim's perspective, it is a resolution of emotional distress within oneself, without the need for change in the other person, or changes in relations (Horwitz 2005). As Conejero (2009) indicates, the victim does not need to have pity or feel empathy toward the person responsible for the pain, nor does this person need to express their apologies or regret in order for the person to be subjectively forgiven. The same author concludes that anger is an obstacle that stops both the victim forgiving the perpetrator as well as the perpetrator asking the victim for forgiveness. On the other hand, perpetrators' apologies and expressions of regret and shame concerning their acts encourages victims to forgive to a greater extent than empathy or compassion.

At both the individual and the group level, the predisposition to offer apologies and to forgive is determined by the subjective assessment of victimization experience, which is in turn determined by the extent to which the aggressor's behavior is considered to be deliberate. The greater the sense of victimization, the less possibility there is of individual forgiveness. The victim fears that granting forgiveness may diminish the recognition of his or her suffering. At a group level, the feeling of victimization reduces the feeling of collective blame; the violent actions of the group itself are easier to justify and they are judged to be less damaging. At the same time, group empathy with the perpetrators reinforces attitudes in favor of forgiveness, while empathy with the victims is made more difficult (Conejero 2009).

Consistent with the results obtained by Miles Hewstone and colleagues (Conejero 2009) in Northern Ireland, the predisposition to forgive ETA—as those responsible for the terrorist acts and damages caused to the victims of Spanish society in its entirety—is closely related to ideologized identity. Identification with one's own group makes it difficult to forgive the actions of the other group. Those who share identity and ideological feelings that are close to those of the terrorist organization ETA share more empathy toward those who they consider to be in their endogroup, and see the perpetrators as victims and the victims as perpetrators or collaborators of the real perpetrators. Under these conditions, and in the short term, it does not make much sense to consider the possibility of mediation and of reconciliation between groups, but instead, the individual expression of apologies on behalf of the perpetrator and the forgiveness of the victims themselves.

Terrorist acts are incomprehensible and unjustifiable for the victims, and negative feelings toward the aggressors do not disappear when justice is enforced. The victim's mind cannot stop trying to understand the reason for the occurrences, to find some meaning out of something that is seen to be without meaning. There is a legitimate case for and a time for hate, pain must be felt, and victims must be able to live satisfactorily with the scars that remain over the healed wounds—scars that are sometimes visible and keep the memory alive. But to forgive and to reconcile oneself cannot be moral imperatives, and never more so than in cases of terrorism. What victims need is to rebuild their sense of security in the notion that terrorist actions will not happen anymore. As a victim of terrorism testifies in Itziar Larizgoitia and colleagues' *La noche de las víctimas*: "At that point I suffered an anxiety attack and I started cursing. I cursed those who had carried it out, I cursed the murderers! Days later I was able to forgive them for what they had done to us in a public letter, now that the pain of loss was so intense that there was no place left for hate" (2009, 68).

Conclusion

More than 50 percent of people have some kind of traumatic experience during their life, and 25 percent have two or more. Victims of political violence suffer distress at a physical, emotional, cognitive, and social level that is greater than that caused by accidents, natural disasters, or other forms of interpersonal violence, and the psychological consequences of political violence are more persistent and difficult to overcome even with psychiatric treatment (Echeburúa 2004). The resilience approach shows that the majority of these people are able to recover and live normal lives without significant health problems several years after the event (Cuesta 2000; Fullerton et al. 2003). Awareness of resilience resources may help to guide victims with more persistent psychological problems. Forgiveness does not necessarily imply forgetting, nor should it be subject to any kind of imposition. It is an individual option available to victims if they find within the process a way to break the self-destructive association with the perpetrator, which hinders their recuperation of psychological well-being.

Considering traumas of a terrorist nature as psychosocial traumas leads us to consider the community dimension of resilience insofar as individual recuperation is linked to a social discourse that dignifies the victims protects them, and contributes toward defeating terrorists.

References

Acinas, Patricia. 2007. "Información a la población en situaciones de emergencia y riesgo colectivo." *Intervención Psicosocial: Revista sobre Igualdad y Calidad de Vida* 16, no. 3: 303–22.

Ararteko: Defensoría del Pueblo. 2009. *Atención institucional a las víctimas del terrorismo en Euskadi: Informe extraordinario de la institución del Ararteko al Parlamento Vasco.* Accessed January 17, 2012. www.ararteko.net.

Baca, Enrique, and María Luisa Cabanas. 1997. "Niveles de salud mental y calidad de vida en las víctimas de terrorismo en España." *Archivos de Neurobiología* 60: 283–96.

Blanco, Amalio, and Dario Díaz. 2004. "Bienestar social y trauma psicosocial: Una visión alernativa al trastorno de estrés postraumático." *Clínica y Salud: Revista de Psicología Clínica y Salud* 15, no. 3: 227–52.

Bleich, Avi, Marc Gelkopf, Yuval Melamed, and Zahava Solomon. 2006. "Mental Health and Resiliency Following 44 Months of Terrorism: A Survey of an Israeli National Representative Sample." *BMC Medicine* 4, no. 21. Accessed January 17, 2012. www.biomedcentral.com/1741-7015/4/21.

Bonanno, George A. 2004. "Loss, Trauma and Human Resilience: Have We Underestimated the Human Capacity to Thrive after Extremely Aversive Events?" *American Psychologist* 59, no. 1: 20–28.

Cabrera, María Luisa, Carlos Martín Beristain, A. Jiménez, and Darío Páez. 2006. "Violencia sociopolítica y cuestionamiento de las creencias básicas sociales." *Psicología Política* 32: 107–30.

Calhoun, Lawrence G., and Richard G. Tedeschi. 1999. *Facilitating Posttraumatic Growth: A Clinician's Guide.* Mahwah, NJ: LEA.

Cano, Antonio, Héctor González, Juan José Miguel, and Itziar Iruarrizaga. 2004. "Los atentados terrorista del 11-M en Madrid: La proximidad de la residencia a las áreas afectadas." *Ansiedad y Estrés* 10, nos. 2–3: 181–94.

Carbelo, Begoña, and Eduardo Jáuregui. 2006. "Emociones positivas: Humor positivo." *Papeles del Psicólogo* 27, no. 1: 18–30.

Colectivo de Víctimas del Terrorismo del País Vasco. "Víctimas mortales de terrorismo." Accessed January 17, 2012. www.covite.org/covite_balancedolor.php.

Conejero, Susana. 2009. "Emociones, actitud hacia el perdón y tolerancia en un contexto de conflicto intergrupal y violencia: El caso vasco." PhD diss., Universidad del País Vasco/Euskal Herriko Unibertsitatea.

Cuesta, Cristina. 2000. *Contra el olvido: Testimonios de víctimas de terrorismo.* Madrid: Temas de Hoy.

Cyrulnik, Boris. 2005. *The Whispering of Ghosts: Trauma and Resilience.* Translated by Susan Fairfield. New York: Other Press.

Durá, Estrella, and Sonia Hernández. 2003. "Los grupos de autoayuda como apoyo social en el cáncer de mama." *Boletín de Psicología* 78: 21–40.

Echeburúa, Enrique. 2004. *Superar un trauma: El tratamiento de las víctimas de sucesos violentos.* Madrid: Pirámide.

———. 2007. "Criterios de actuación en el tratamiento psicológico de las víctimas de terrorismo." *Infocoponline: Revista de Psicología* 32. Accessed January 17, 2012. www.cop.es/infocop/vernumero.asp?id=1455.

Echeburúa, Enrique, Paz de Corral, and Pedro Javier Amor. 2002. "Evaluación del daño psicológico en las víctimas de delitos violentos." *Psicothema* 14 (Suppl.): 139–46.

Francart, Loup. 2010. "What Does Resilience Really Mean?" Accessed January 17, 2012. www.diploweb.com/What-does-resilence-really-mean.html.

Fullerton, Carol S., Robert J. Ursano, Ann E. Norwood, and Harry H. Holloway. 2003. "Trauma, Terrorism and Disaster." In *Terrorism and Disaster: Individual and Community Mental Health Interventions,* edited by Robert J. Ursano, Carol S. Fullerton, and Ann E. Norwood. Cambridge: Cambridge University Press.

Ganzel, Barbara, B. J. Casey, Gary Glover, Henning U. Voss, and Elise Temple. 2007. "The Aftermath of 9/11: Effect of Intensity and Recency of Trauma on Outcome." *Emotion* 7, no. 2: 227–38.

Grotberg, Edith H. 2002. "From Terror to Triumph: The Path to Resilience." In *The Psychology of Terrorism: Coping with the Continuing Threat*, edited by Chris E. Stout. Westport, CT: Praeger.

Hobfoll, Steven E., Patrick A. Palmieri, Robert J. Johnson, Daphna Canetti-Nisim, Brian J. Hall, and Sandro Galea. 2009. "Trajectories of Resilience, Resistance and Distress during Ongoing Terrorism: The Case of Jews and Arabs in Israel." *Journal of Consulting and Clinical Psychology* 77, no. 1: 138–48.

Horwitz, Leonard. 2005. "The Capacity to Forgive: Intrapsychic and Developmental Perspectives." *Journal of the American Psychoanalytic Association* 53, no. 2: 485–511.

Larizgoitia, Itziar, Isabel Izarzugaza, and Iñaki Markez. 2009. *La noche de las víctimas: Investigación sobre el Impacto en la Salud de la Violencia Colectiva (ISAVIC) en el País Vasco*. Bilbao: Fundación Fernando Buesa Blanco Fundazioa.

Lima, María de la Luz. 2006. "Las víctimas del delito y el abuso del poder del terrorismo." *Eguzkilore: Cuaderno del Instituto Vasco de Criminología* 20: 41–73.

López, Andrés Fernando, Alexis Kasanzew, and María Soledad Fernández. 2008. "Los efectos psicoterapéuticos de estimular la connotación positiva en el incremento del perdón." *Avances en Psicología Latinoamericana* 26, no. 2: 211–26.

Llera, Francisco J., and Alfredo Retortillo. 2005. *Los españoles y las víctimas del terrorismo: 1ª encuesta nacional "percepción ciudadana sobre las víctimas del terrorismo en España."* Madrid: CIS.

Maeseele, Pieter A., Gino Verleye, Isabelle Stevens, and Anne Speckhard. 2008. "Psychosocial Resilience in the Face of a Mediated Terrorist Threat." *Media, War & Conflict* 1, no. 1: 50–69.

Maguire, Brigit, and Sophie Cartwright. 2008. "Assessing a Community's Capacity to Manage Change: A Resilience Approach to Social Assessment." Australian Government, Bureau of Rural Sciences. Accessed January 17, 2012. http://adl.brs.gov.au/brsShop/html/brs_prod_90000004076.html.

Martín, Carlos, and Darío Páez. 2000. *Violencia, apoyo a las víctimas y reconstrucción social: Experiencias internacionales y el desafío vasco.* Madrid: Fundamentos.

Nemeroff, Charles B., J. Douglas Bremner, Edna B. Foa, Helen S. Mayberg, Carol S. North, and Murray B. Stein. 2006. "Post-Traumatic

Stress Disorder: A State-of-Science Review." *Journal of Psychiatric Research* 40: 1–21.

Páez, Darío, Itziar Fernández, and Carlos Martín. 2001. "Catástrofes, traumas y conductas colectivas: Procesos y efectos culturales." In *Catástrofes y ayuda de emergencia: Estrategias de evaluación, prevención y tratamiento*, edited by César San Juan. Barcelona: Icaria.

Pérez Esquivel, Adolfo. 2000. Prologue to *Violencia, apoyo a las víctimas y reconstrucción social: Experiencias internacionales y el desafío vasco*, by Carlos Martín Beristaín and Darío Paéz. Madrid: Fundamentos.

Pfefferbaum, Betty J., Dori B. Reissman, Rose L. Pfefferbaum, Richard W. Klomp, and Robin H. Gurwitch. 2007. "Building Resilience to Mass Trauma Events." In *Handbook of Injury and Violence Prevention*, edited by Lynda S. Doll, Sandra E. Bonzo, James A. Mercy, and David A. Sleet. New York: Springer.

Rimé, Bernard, Dario Páez, and Francisco Martínez. 2004. "Los efectos del comportamiento social de las emociones sobre el trauma del 11 de Marzo en personas no afectadas directamente." *Ansiedad y Estrés* 10, nos. 2–3: 219–32.

San Juan, César. 2001. "La intervención en desastres: Bases conceptuales y operativas." In *Catástrofes y ayuda de emergencia*, edited by César San Juan. Barcelona: Icaria.

Schmid, Alex P., and Albert I. Jongman, with the collaboration of Michael Stohl et al. 1988. *Political Terrorism: A New Guide to Actors, Authors, Concepts, Data Bases, Theories and Literature*. Foreword by I. L. Horowitz. Amsterdam: SWIDOC; Transaction Books.

Strelan, Peter, N. T. Feather, and Ian Mckee. 2008. "Justice and Forgiveness: Experimental Evidence for Compatibility." *Journal of Experimental Social Psychology* 44, no. 6: 1538–44.

Suárez-Ojeda, Elbio Néstor, Ana María de la Fara, and Claudia V. Márquez. 2007. "Trabajo comunitario y resiliencia social." In *Adolescencia y resiliencia*, edited by Mabel M. Munist, Elbio Néstor Suárez-Ojeda, Dina Krauskopf, and Tomás José Silber. Buenos Aires: Paidós.

Twigg, John. 2007. *Characteristics of a Disaster-resilient Community: A Guidance Note*. Accessed January 17, 2012. http://practicalaction.org/reducing-vulnerability/docs/ia1/community-characteristics-en-lowres.pdf.

Uriarte, Juan de D. 2005. "La resiliencia: Una nueva perspectiva en psicopatología del desarrollo." *Revista de Psicodidáctica* 10, no. 2: 61–80.

———. 2010. "La resiliencia comunitaria en situaciones catastróficas y de emergencia." *INFAD: Revista de Psicología/International Journal of Developmental and Educational Psychology* 1, no. 1: 275–82.

Vazquez, Carmelo. 2005. "Stress Reactions of the General Population after the Terrorist Attacks of S11, 2001 (USA) and M11, 2004 (Madrid, Spain): Myths and Realities." *Annuary of Clinical and Health Psychology* 1: 9–25.

Vázquez, Carmelo, Pau Pérez-Sales, and Georg Matt. 2006. "Post-Traumatic Stress Reactions following the March 11, 2004 Terrorist Attacks in a Madrid Community Sample: A Cautionary Note about the Measurement of Psychological Trauma." *Spanish Journal of Psychology* 9, no. 1: 61–74.

Vera, Beatriz. 2004. "Resistir y rehacerse: Una reconceptualización de la experiencia traumática desde la psicología positiva." *Revista de Psicología Positiva* 1. Accessed January 17, 2012. www.psicologia-positiva.com.

Vera, Beatriz, Begoña Carbelo, and María Luisa Vecina. 2006. "La experiencia traumática desde la psicología positiva: Resiliencia y crecimiento traumático." *Papeles del Psicólogo* 27, no. 1: 40–49.

Verleye, Gino, Pieter Maeseele, Isabelle Stevens, and Anne Speckhard. 2008. "Resilience in an Age of Terrorism: Psychology, Media and Communication" Prepublication copy. Accessed January 17, 2012. www.annespeckhard.com/publications/Resilience_in_an_Age_of_Terrorism_Psychology_Media_and_Communication.pdf.

Wade, Nathaniel G., Donna C. Bailey, and Philip Shaffer. 2005. "Helping Clients Heal: Does Forgiveness Make a Difference?" *Professional Psychology: Research and Practice* 36, no. 6: 634–41.

Walsh, Froma. 2007. "Traumatic Loss and Major Disasters: Strengthening Family and Community Resilience." *Family Process* 46, no. 2: 207–27.

Wenzel, Michael, and Tyler G. Okimoto. 2010. "How Acts of Forgiveness Restore a Sense of Justice: Addressing Status/Power and Value Concerns Raised by Transgressions." *European Journal of Social Psychology* 40, no. 3: 401–17.

7

Getting Closer: Photography, Death, and Terrorist Violence in the Basque Country

Ramón Esparza and Nekane Parejo

Translated by Jennifer Martin

On January 24, 2010, the newspaper *El País* published extensive coverage in its central booklet on an event that until that time, very few people apart from those directly involved had knowledge of. The history of the ETA assassinations actually began eight years before the assassination of civil guard Pardines in 1968. The first victim was named Begoña Urroz Ibarrola, who died when she was only twenty-two months old, completely burned by the explosion of a bomb placed in the Amara train station in San Sebastián on June 27, 1960. Thus a new name needed to be added, this time at the beginning, to the long list of the 857 people assassinated until today.[1]

The newspaper report cited the book *Vidas rotas* (Broken Lives), (Alonso, Domínguez, and García Rey 2010) as the source in which the

---

* This text assembles some of the conclusions drawn by Nekane Parejo in her doctoral thesis *Photography and Death: The Graphic Representation of ETA Attacks (1968–1997)*, directed by Ramón Esparza and defended at the University of the Basque Country in 2003. Ramón Esparza, a press photographer during the period 1976–1987, before becoming a university professor, bore witness as a photographer to part of the events whose representation is studied here and is the author of some of the images.

1. Actually, the death of Begoña Urroz from an ETA attack was already known, although it was not publicly disclosed. In her doctoral thesis, defended in 2002, Nekane Parejo specifically mentioned the fact, and additionally pointed out the total lack of information on this event apart from the Ministry of the Interior's concise official notes.

lives and deaths of all the victims were briefly recounted, in an impressive compilation of more than 1,300 pages. Strangely enough, the book still began the long list with José Pardines, assassinated on July 7, 1968, when he detained a vehicle in which two members of the recently created ETA were traveling, Iñaki Sarasketa and Francisco Javier Etxebarrieta. The mention of the little girl's death appeared separate from the list, as if it had been a last-minute investigation. The event was attributed to the Directorio Revolucionario Ibérico de Liberación (DRIL, or the Iberian Revolutionary Liberation Directorate) for a long time, and ETA had never been recognized as the perpetrator, even though in 1992 a mention of it was found in the computer records of José Luis Álvarez Santacristina, Txelis, after he was arrested in Bidart. There were only a few lines in the press at that time that told of the event and the funeral service.

The secrecy imposed on this fact by both ETA and Franco's government permitted reflection on terrorism and nondemocratic regimes along with the concept of visibility. Maintaining silence on the girl's death suited both sides for opposing reasons. It helped ETA achieve the disastrous (although predictable) outcomes of its June 1960 placement of explosive devices in train stations in Barcelona and Donostia–San Sebastián, and in a train running through the Zaragoza province at the time of explosion. For Franco's government, which only released a brief statement recounting the events on the following day and attributed them to "terrorist orders that foreign elements, in cooperation with separatists and Spanish communists, have been strongly advocating," the silence helped to deny the existence of political opposition movements with sufficient infrastructure to attack concrete objectives. For once, both sides coincided in their desire for invisibility, validating the expression known in the communication world: no picture, no news.

Visibility regulation is a basic characteristic of totalitarian regimes. One the one hand, the political system denies the rights of citizens to maintain their own areas of invisibility (the intimacy of one's home, a private life), seeking to become a panoptical system, as described by Michel Foucault, in which nothing remains hidden from state supervision. On the other hand, that same system hides or declares its opposition's activities invisible, preventing it from becoming public knowledge and obtaining greater support.

Terrorism also has its own regime of visibility. As Fernando Reinares pointed out (1993, 48), given its clandestine nature, terrorism adopts the necessary measures for its safeguard, mainly based on its invisibility as an organization (its members and structure are unknown to security forces) and on its structure's compartmentalization. Terrorist organizations simultaneously build visibility through violent actions and their dissemination through the media. Jean Baudrillard clearly stated this problem in his reflections on 9/11, affirming, "Terrorism would be nothing without the media" (2002, 414).

The entrance of this third element in the visibility game of politically motivated violence is a recurring subject of debate in democratic societies, since it puts the media in the awkward position of having to avoid the temptation to suppress news and contribute to the end goals of the terrorist act. The position of the media regarding this matter has always been complicated. Terrorism has evolved toward increasingly violent and dramatic actions, with the purpose of attracting media attention (Keinan, Sadeh, and Rosen 2003, 150). At the same time, the media have developed organizational structures during the past thirty years that allow them to respond to the current, immediate demand that news on terrorism always constitutes. Events of this nature have their own characteristics of a news event at its highest level: lack of foresight, violence, drama, and effects on society.

Logically, an image is the most effective communication support for the two poles of terrorist activity, given that the pursued objectives are emotional in character. One only needs to consider the case of Begoña Urroz to realize that. There was not even one picture that could tell us about the explosion that took a life that had only just begun. There was no written information either, apart from the Ministry of the Interior's concise official notes. The newspaper *El País* only managed, upon journalistically discovering the case, to publish a photo of the parents holding the little girl. It was the only visual image, albeit indirect, of an event that had remained unknown until then. Invisible.

Eleven years later, Tom Hopkinson (1971, 7) defended the photographic medium in a society in which television began to mark its territory by contending that press photography was the first medium to bring ordinary people into direct visual contact with the world around them. Hopkinson pointed out that the media's publication of photographs allows citizens to see the aspect of things for themselves, including the features of important people of their time and places that they would never visit. The primary function of photography in the press is not, however, that innocent vision that Hopkinson proposed, but something much more sophisticated. Its use is determined by a series of decisions based on guidelines more or less assimilated from professional ideology and business, commercial, political, and ideological interests. Harold Evans summarized it in the first sentence of the introduction to his book *Pictures on a Page*: "The camera cannot lie, but it can be an accessory to untruth" (1978). He then enumerated the different stages of an image's discursive process to encase that which is represented in the general story of the events as told by the media: the necessary selection made by the photographer and the graphic editor; the *guidance* that the caption below the photo provides; and finally, the interpretive work of the reader him/herself. The photos in the media do not put readers in contact with the world in which they live, as Hopkinson declared. Rather, they contribute to creating a visual world or a vision of that world, one in which certain elements are abundantly shown while others remain in the shadows.

Accepting the idea of a visible cultural dimension entails the acceptance of the invisible. An invisibility that could have several motives: biological, moral, social, and political. The photographic camera and its derivatives (film and television) have played a central role in that process of constructing the visible during the past two centuries. But, as we have seen, its explanation cannot just take its technological characteristics into account, forgetting its discursive overlap. It may be that the camera is a neutral element, but its use is culturally determined, making it part of a much more complex phenomenon than the simple reproduction of a fragment of the historical world: the construction of a scopic regime.

Starting from the idea of Michel Foucault's "epistemological order" (1994), authors such as Donald M. Lowe (1982), Martin Jay (1988), and Allen Feldman (1997) developed the concept of scopic regime, assuming that in the regulation of our worldview there was a series of rules or unconscious presuppositions that historically changed.

Contemplating a photographic image as a simple reproduction or representation of an event involves forgetting the ideological connotations, not of the principle technique by which the image is created, but of the whole cultural process that ranges from choosing a representational model to selecting what is shown, or not, and how it is shown. It was not purely by chance that there were no images of the attack on the Amara station. One only needs to look at the newspapers of that time to realize that. On Tuesday, January 28, 1960, the newspapers published a photo of Franco handing the Generalissimo's Cup (a soccer tournament) to the captain of Atlético Madrid, the winner of that year. Simply browsing through that edition and those from the following and previous days offers an immediate lesson. Franco, or elements from his political regime, such as religious symbols or the army, habitually occupied the front pages of some newspapers that hid, more voluntarily than forcibly, large portions of what was really happening. The guidelines of journalism's professional ideology were subject to an agenda firmly marked by censorship from the regime.

The continuation of attacks resulting in death after Franco's rule ended led to the reactivation of those professional guidelines and a struggle to change the scopic regime, especially after Franco's death in 1975. Democracy was understood, in the communication field, as the right to know and, consequently, the right to see.

The formation of that right had several facets. The first of those, logically, was a reformulation of the country's social and political freedoms, a process that would not be fully achieved until many years after Franco's death. It wasn't just a matter of formal liberties, consecrated in the constitution, but also of their *social* acceptance, by the citizens as well as by the lower echelons of power. Parallel to this acceptance was the pressure of society as a whole toward a broader scope of vision and the development of professional guidelines and strategies on the part of photojournalists that would allow it. For a press accustomed to following the government's directives, the development of mechanisms that enabled a quick response in the face of a totally unforeseen event like a terrorist attack involved the acceptance of new professional guidelines, the search for sources that provided quick knowledge of the facts, and professionals capable of responding immediately.

The process was visible in the progression from the total invisibility of Begoña Urroz's assassination to the representation of those that occurred in the last years of Franco's dictatorship and the beginning of democracy. It was the slow configuration of what, in structuralist terms, we could call a narrative model, if it were not for the macabre end result: the presentation of a person's violent death.

The death of Guardia Civil member José Pardines in Villabona (June 7, 1968)[2] was treated with the same invisibility as that of Begoña Urroz, although the media were aware of the fact. The first visual coverage of an attack was published for the assassination of Melitón Manzanas in August of that same year. It included a passport-sized photo of the deceased,

---

2. The dates between parentheses correspond to the execution of the attacks of each victim discussed here.

another of the house that he had lived in, and a third image of the stairs with an arrow pointing to the spot where the assailant hid and waited for the victim. On the following day, the Basque Country newspapers published overviews of the funeral and the burial.

Macabre iconography of the attacks was slowly actualized with the incorporation of new elements. In the death of taxi driver Fermín Monasterio, the images mainly focused on the burial by showing a long shot of those attending and friends of the deceased bearing the coffin. They were still long shots, taken from far away, though, and therefore expressionless, which reported the ceremony as a rite of passage, without appealing to the more humanist rhetoric: the expression of strong emotions. The low quality of the photographs' printed reproduction, along with their small size and the visual sterility that they exhibited, resulted in an ambiguous interpretation, and if the photos spoke of anything, it was of absence. The absence of the victim, who was only visually affirmed through the presence of the casket, was foremost. But there was also the absence of the supposedly shown facts, those that only the graphic processing of the image, with the inclusion of arrows or circles, made reference to.

The reason for this remoteness could be found in the strict censorship of Franco's regime and its implications for the professional ideology. Publio López Mondéjar (1997, 180) spoke of a professional majority "anchored in excessively refined decorative work . . . that agreed so much with the objectives of a regime that sought to hide the country's reality."

Despite that, the newspapers developed their professional guidelines and achieved, if not direct images of the attacks (that the censorship would never have allowed to be published), at least other images that alluded to the victim and other victims (people in their family and social circle) in an indirect way. In addition to the identification photo, they added other photos from a family album, like the one from the first communion of civil guard Eloy Garcia's youngest son (December 29, 1972).[3] Nondescript shots of the attack site were also taken once all of the investigation items were taken away. The only sphere of activity that was left to the photojournalist was the funeral, in which he or she could show the official version of the ceremony, with the authorities in the first row of the church, the transfer of the casket, and the visual element in which

---

3. One element that was always present in photographers' bags during this period was a powerful telephoto lens that allowed them to take a shot of the photo from the victim's professional identification badge.

the social impact of the camera's raw power was expressed: the widow. She was shocked, stunned by the situation, and supported by family or friends, a central element of the ceremony in its original significance (the farewell to someone that has died), but nevertheless displaced from the center by the institutional weight. The widow could not go unseen. She could not decline to be photographed, exposed in her pain to the eyes of others, and once the funeral rites and burial were completed, she was plunged into solitude.[4]

The first attack that received extensive visual coverage (even the state television gave it wide coverage) was the assassination of then government president Luis Carrero Blanco. It was an act with too much public interest (a bomb placed on a centrally located street in Madrid) and too many political consequences (in fact, it produced a change of course in the final years of Franco's dictatorship) to be treated discreetly.

The national newspapers opened their edition on the following day with expanded graphic coverage. The official photo of the victim was first and foremost. It was an image not only that gave an impression of what had occurred but also that conferred authority on the matter. The photos of the site (as always, the journalists arrived late), with the enormous gap left by the explosion or the official car in the Jesuits' building's inner courtyard on Claudio Coello street, were placed, in the *ABC* newspaper for example, on inner pages, mixed with the Christmas-season advertisements. As far as the Basque Country newspapers were concerned, they reproduced the ruling vision, including photos of Carrero Blanco's public activities. The central theme in all the newspapers was the enormous hole the explosion made, but photos of locals in the area carrying off personal belongings were also included, and for the first time the funeral chapel, with the open casket, that permitted one to contemplate the victim's face. The attack on Carrero Blanco was the first to bring an end to the visual representation scheme of such attacks.

But despite that, the images continued to have an overall note of weakness and remoteness (physical as well as discursive), reinforced by the poor print quality. The difficulties imposed on the journalists' work,

---

4. Many times fiction is capable of transmitting emotions in a much more efficient way than the truest of tales. In several of his short stories, Fernando Aramburu (2006) described the bitterness and the solitude of those who, in addition to having lost one of their own to a violent death, had to live with the denial of some and the forgetfulness of others. The terrible phrase "something must be done" became more of a self-excuse than a common cause.

the lack of professional encouragement, and a great awareness of those limitations resulted in a bureaucratic-style photography of deserted scenes in which not even the slightest indication of what had happened existed and to which it was necessary to add arrows and all types of explanations in order to turn them into news items. There was not even a trace of the emotional component.

The change in this situation came, if you'll excuse the repetition, with change. Franco's death and the opening of the stormy passage toward democracy brought with it the appearance of new publications, daily newspapers as well as weeklies, and of new professionals with ideas and approaches that were very different from those already in the trade. These new faces were willing to challenge the restrictions imposed on their work and to assume the risks that the job entailed. The first newspaper of the democracy, *El País*, was founded in 1976, and a year later the publication of two new papers began in the Basque Country: *Deia*, associated with the Basque Nationalist Party (EAJ-PNV by its Basque and Spanish acronyms), and *Egin*, which was the left *abertzale* (radical left-wing Basque nationalism). The new media's photographers were professionals with new ideological guidelines, more in line with journalistic principles such as those practiced in other countries, which developed professional strategies that allowed them to respond with the immediacy needed in the face of an unforeseen attack.

The result, at the visual level, was the progressive population of the crime scene, in which witnesses, family members, emergency service workers, and law enforcement began to appear, until finally arriving at the inclusion of the corpse and the reduction of the remoteness used in the report. There was no longer a long shot of a deserted scene that would later be filled in with diagrams and labels.

The appearance of the victim in the picture involved important changes in professional routines as well as in the attitude of the authorities. The first changes involved turning to new informative sources (generally emergency medical services that established a symbiosis with the media in which they exchanged information for visibility); the second ones entailed granting access to the crime scene little by little, increasing the visibility level of terrorist acts.

The first image of this type was published in *La Gaceta del Norte* after the assassination of taxi driver Manuel Albizu (March 16, 1976). All the information that until then had to be placed in a caption under the photo, or shown by the confusing arrows, was now displayed, harshly and directly, in the photo in which we saw the body of the taxi driver seated in his car, with two trails of blood coming out of his head, which was leaning forward. Another image of this type would not be published again for some time. It was the body of Javier de Ybarra in the Basurto hospital morgue in Bilbao, where he was sent after being found dead on the summit of Barázar, near Bilbao. The entry point of the bullet in his right temple could be seen in the photo. The publication of this and other similar images in several papers caused some tensions given that de Ybarra's family owned one of the local newspapers was part of the business elite in Bizkaia, and because of the unusualness of the photo itself. Obtained surreptitiously, without the explicit permission of the authorities, the photo was a sign of a new approach to journalism, one that explicitly broke with accommodating the directives originating from the previous regime and censorship. However, the photo's publication also had implications of another type. From that moment on, the media began to be governed by their own professional rules. They engaged in competition with one another, and as they did, the power of the camera became clear, along with the ideal of a transparent modern society, in which everything must be seen and in which the media had the role of arbitrating between their own members through, in this case, images and text. The visibility principle was superimposed above others, such as that of the victim's privacy and integrity.

On November 29, 1977, the papers published news of the assassination of the head of the Policía Armada (Armed Police) in Iruñea-Pamplona, accompanied by an image that, with slight variations, would come to be an iconographic model: the body on the ground, the pool of blood, the blanket that was covering it pushed aside, and the harsh light of the camera's flash that made the scene appear highly contrasted against an almost always black background.

Along with the faster response time, the new print media introduced news values that had not been taken into account until then. The inclusion of the human factor, the representation of emotions, moods, pain, rage, fear, and despondency made the readers connect much more with what the photos captured. In the information about the funeral of Augusto Unceta (October 8, 1977), who was assassinated in Gernika with two bodyguards, the newspaper *Deia* published a series of images that focused on the emotional reactions of the attendees instead of a picture of the crowd or the coffins in the church, as was common under the previous authorities.[5] Readers saw the tension reflected in the faces of the family of the guards that escorted Unceta, the sadness on the face of one of the widows holding her daughter of eight months, and the anger on the face of one of the attendees that rebuked the political representatives. The graphic coverage of events went from being built by a series of micro-histories to being elevated to the category of news.

The Years of Lead

Terrorist activity reached its highest intensity in the final years of the 1970s and the beginning of the 1980s. They were years in which an attack occurred every few days and sometimes two in the same day. The media's frenetic pace led to a sort of professional madness, in which tough competition was established, not only in being the first to arrive on the scene but also in capturing the hardest-hitting photo. And for that, there was no lack of subjects. The assassins reached their victims inside their cars (Lisardo Sampil, December 31, 1978), in the middle of the street (Heliodoro Arriaga, November 28, 1978), in public places such as bars (Vincente Ereño, December 6, 1978), or in their workplace (Juan Jiménez, December 14, 1978), and the photographers captured the scene as clearly and directly as possible. Lifting the blanket or sheet that covered the body was the norm, as the differences between photos published by different papers on the same day and the usual presence of blankets or sheets by the side of the body demonstrated. The elements that displayed the full intensity of drama—such as the pools of blood covered with sawdust, bodies with mouths still open or thrown into a ditch—became part of everyday practice. The camera and its flash acted as a barrier that protected the photographer from the emotional impact of the scene and permitted him to focus on getting the image that was guaranteed to be on the front page, putting news value above moral values. Photographers, as Susan Sontag (1977) pointed out, assumed a noninterventionist stance, which is nothing but a nonreflective stance.

One of the flash points of this process was marked by the death of an engineer from the electric company Iberduero, who during those years was working on the construction of a nuclear power plant near Bilbao.

---

5. For example, see the October 11 edition in which the graphic coverage was limited to a large image of the Guardia Civil escorting the caskets, together with Unceta's widow and the mother of one of the guards entering the church.

The environmental opposition quickly turned into political opposition, and ETA declared a fight against the construction of the plant. After several attacks on the construction site, José María Ryan, the project's chief engineer, was kidnapped on January 29, 1981. Following the release of a statement that urged the government to demolish the plant within seven days, Ryan was assassinated on February 6. His body appeared abandoned by the side of a forest road in the municipality of Zaratamo (Bizkaia), with his hands bound and a shot to the back of his head.

The photo coverage in the newspapers the next day was the usual: images of the location where he turned up and a close-up of the body on the ground with a white handkerchief covering his eyes. The only difference appeared in *Deia*, in which the scene could be viewed more completely: the body lying on the ground, the police who had found the site, and the photographers crammed together around the corpse, even placing themselves astride it in order to get a close-up of the face. The scene was more completely understood, and the halo of testimony deflated when a wider angle was used. Any references to the difficulty, the harshness, of getting up in the middle of the night to go to an incident's site, on the effort to comply with photojournalism's maxim—to be there so that the readers could see it—no longer worked. The photographer was there to attain a valuable object: the image of the tragedy.

The rate of deaths and macabre images on the newspapers' front pages continued however during the 1980s. A month later (March 5, 1981), ETA returned to killing. This time it was a police commissioner in Bilbao, and they would kill another twenty-six times during that year. Meanwhile, the military coup that was attempted on February 23 complicated the situation even more.

But a new factor entered the scene in 1982 that carried the threshold of what was visible on the newspapers' front pages even further. That year ETA began to use explosives in their attacks, achieving far greater, and above all, much more spectacular effects with them. Explosives had previously been used, but not on that scale. An attack with a car bomb or other similar means also managed to boost the psychological effect. While shots were directed at a person, who was later blamed in the subsequent communiqué, a bomb was indiscriminate, killing whoever was around it. In any given moment, everyone could be a victim. The spreading of terrorist acts outside of the Basque Country further strengthened this objective while still granting greater impunity to the perpetrators since they could remain several feet away from the attack site and escape undetected.

A bomb placed underneath a car took the life of Guardia Civil captain Luis Ollo (May 27, 1984), while an action of even greater relevance took place against a convoy of army vehicles transporting soldiers back home. A car bomb placed on the shoulder of the road in El Gallo, near Galdakao (Bizkaia), destroyed a minibus carrying fourteen soldiers, killing one and injuring the rest. Two others died in the hospital shortly thereafter. The following year, a car bomb in a shopping center parking lot caused the death of Esteban del Amo (June 12, 1985), the explosives expert who tried to deactivate it. Thirteen months later (July 14, 1986), a car bomb destroyed a Guardia Civil bus in Madrid's Plaza of the Dominican Republic, causing nine deaths and numerous wounded. The site of the attack (in the very center of Madrid) caused an enormous media reaction. The following day's photos showed the police aiding their comrades, pulling them away from the attack site without any means other than their own hands, among flames and the scattered remnants of the bus.

One year later (June 19, 1987), a car bomb placed in an underground parking garage of the Hipercor superstore in Barcelona exploded at 4:10 in the afternoon. The terrorists had notified several local media sources and the Guardia Urbana (local police) in Barcelona, but those responsible for the shopping center did not believe that evacuation was necessary. Twenty-one people died and another forty-five were injured in that explosion, one of ETA's bloodiest attacks. The difficult rescue of the victims and, once again, the location of the attack, in the middle of Barcelona's Meridiana Avenue, meant that the media arrived at the site to witness the full chaos of firefighters, emergency services, and ambulances. The images were of charred bodies and the injured lying on stretchers. In Zaragoza (December 11, 1987), terrorists placed an explosive charge in a car parked next to a Guardia Civil housing block. Eleven people died; five little girls, daughters of the guards, were among them. A year and a half later (April 29, 1991) another bomb destroyed the Vic barracks in Catalonia, causing the death of ten people and considerable injuries to twenty-eight others. The attack's target was, without a doubt, the guards' families, in a clear attempt to reinforce the feeling of indiscriminate terror. The media printed images on the following day that displayed what happened in all its brutality (and symbolism): a guard, with his face bloodied, carried a little girl in his arms while another guard, equally covered in blood, tried to console his wife. She was pushing a stroller, in which their little boy sat smiling, oblivious to what had occurred. Smoke, debris, and ravaged cars surrounded both scenes.

The brutality of the attacks in the second half of the 1980s, with indiscriminate deaths, destruction, and chaos, undoubtedly reached the visual policy's maximum extent, in which the idea of transparency bordered on the obscene.[6] From the 1990s onward, the media and photographers began to take a backward step with regard to what was shown in images (Parejo 2004, 433). It was not a return to the 1970s situation, in which the political framework imposed a visual regime that decreed its symbols omnipresent and anything that did not reinforce its ideology was invisible. In this case we are talking about a moderation of the previous years' excesses and a reflection on the image's role in the media, understood as twofold device.

Theorists critical of the perspective presented a model of the camera's image as a power relation, in which the observer assumes an active position, the *ability to look*, while the observed maintains a passive attitude of *being looked at*. But in this relationship, the rights of the passive subjects concerning their images were not considered. They did not get to decide if they wanted to be looked at. And in the scopic regime of violence, the camera was not only an instrument to take pictures with but also a weapon itself. To be photographed, to have your photograph published in a newspaper, posed a real risk. It was a risk for members of security forces that could become targets of terrorist acts, as well as for those who constituted the terrorists' legal support base (Feldman 1997, 29). At the end of the 1980s, newspaper photos began to feature black strips covering the eyes of security force members in an attempt to reconcile the right to information and the protection of privacy.

What nobody spoke of until now was the location of the victims (the deceased, the wounded, and their relatives) in relation to the image. The vision of the body of a husband, father, or spouse lying on the ground with a large pool of blood underneath—or later, blown up by the explosion of a car bomb, or the close-up with a trickle of blood coming from the side of the head—questioned the limits on the right to privacy and the media's respect for them.

It was not an easy question, nor did it exclusively involve photographers, who for the most part were caught up in a spiral promoted by their own companies that pushed them to take a more spectacular photo.

---

6. A few linguists assert that the word derives from the Latin *cenum*, or mud, but the accepted version is the one that D. H. Lawrence used, *obscenum*, outside the scene: that which should not be seen but that one imagines.

The majority of the professionals thought that the photographer's job was, above all, to capture the image. To publish it or not was another question that corresponded to the media, and they needed to consider aspects such as the fact that one of terrorism's objectives rested precisely in its actions achieving a wide impact. According to Walter Laqueur, "The media are a terrorist's best friend" (Schmid 1989, 539), and the escalation in car bombs at the end of the 1980s produced a highly negative media effect for a society that began to show signs of having had enough of terrorism. It was finally the market itself, society, who decided what they wanted and did not want to see: "The spectacle of terrorism imposes the terrorism of the spectacle. . . . There is no good use of the media: the media is part of the event itself, part of the terror, and its role plays in both directions" (Baudrillard 2002, 414).

"The fact that the readers are averse to harsh images is a key factor in reducing the presence of violent photos. Above all if the victims are close together," stated the graphic editor of *El Correo* (Parejo 2004, 489). In the beginning of the 1990s a progressive distancing was observed in photographs with respect to the place of the occurrence (Parejo 2004). A physical distancing, but above all, an expository distancing took place. The photos were taken from farther away and the body appeared out of focus, but it also tended to be covered by a sheet that was not pushed off to the side now. *El Correo* (November 8, 1991) published a photograph in which a forensic police officer was photographing the cadaver of a little boy, Fabián Moreno, while someone helped him lift the sheet. The photo showed the complete scene, without seeking to focus on the child's face. A new iconography gradually replaced the harshness of the photos from the 1980s. Images that now made up the representation of the attack included the sterile vision of the scene, a vehicle destroyed in a carbomb attack, a policeman with his back to the camera contemplating the place in which his fellow officer was assassinated, the specialists inspecting the spot where the victim was found, and the wounded (not the dead).

Another element to consider was the inclusion of color, along with the increased realism that it brought. Now, the bloodstains were not a dark stain on the ground or on the faces of the wounded. They were red. And if the black and white had lent a certain drama to the scene, color added a degree of impact that was hard to bear.

But the change in the readers' attitude was not limited to rejecting images that were too violent. Little by little, first in small groups that had to courageously face the intimidation of other groups in favor of ETA (the scopic regime of violence again), later in greater numbers, the citizens of the Basque Country began to react to the violence and a new iconographic model appeared: signs of rejection. This was seen in the crowds that attended the funerals, the long lines in the funeral chapels, and the outraged gatherings. This could be seen in the reactions to the assassination of Gregorio Ordóñez, councilman from the Partido Popular (People's Party, PP) in the Donostia-San Sebastián city hall on January 24, 1995, and that of Francisco Tomás y Valiente, on February 14, 1996, from which the symbol of the white hands emerged. Thousands of students demonstrated in Madrid's universities by raising their hands, painted white, in a show of condemnation for the assassination of the professor and former member of the Constitutional Court.

But where the rejection became a human tide, peaceful but uncontrolled, was in the reaction to the death of Ermua (Bizkaia) councilman Miguel Ángel Blanco. In its refined terrorist tactic, ETA assumed that its media goals, its visibility, would be accomplished as before, with greater intensity even, by choosing its objectives from among the rank and file of the political parties. The leaders were not the only possible objectives now: any councilman, any rank and file, could be assassinated because of his or her political affiliation. Miguel Ángel Blanco (July 27, 1997) was one of the first objectives chosen. ETA kidnapped him at noon one day as he was riding the train to work and asked for the immediate transfer of prisoners from its organization to Basque Country jails. After two days, the deadline given to comply with the demand, Blanco turned up in a clearing in the municipal of Lasarte (Gipuzkoa), critically injured with two bullet wounds to the head.

The people's reaction was immediate, with mass gatherings in Ermua during the two days of the futile wait. The images in which the demonstrators carried candles and the text "Miguel, we are waiting for you" were repeated in all the newspapers on the days prior to the assassination. Photos of his parents and sister also figured prominently. After the assassination, the photos were of the massive funeral turnout and the demonstrations organized in all the Basque Country capitals. The images related to Blanco's assassination—the location where he was found and the stretcher entering the emergency room at the hospital in Donostia-San Sebastián—were moved to the background in favor of those that showed the reaction of the people. With that, we can say, the cycle was brought to a close, and the corpse that occupied the front pages of the newspapers for so many years vanished.

References

Alonso, Rogelio, Florencio Domínguez, and Marcos García Rey. 2010. *Vidas rotas.* Madrid: Espasa.

Aramburu, Fernando. 2006. *Los peces de la amargura.* Barcelona: Tusquets.

Baudrillard, Jean. 2002. "L'esprit du terrorisme." *South Atlantic Quarterly* 101, no. 2: 403–15.

Evans, Harold. 1978. *Pictures on a Page: Photo-Journalism, Graphics and Picture Editing.* New York: Holt, Reinhart, and Winston.

Feldman, Allen. 1997. "Violence and Vision: Prosthetics and Aesthetics of Terror." *Public Culture* 10, no. 1: 24–60.

Foucault, Michel. 1994. *The Order of Things: An Archaeology of the Human Sciences.* New York: Vintage Books.

Hopkinson, Tom. 1971. *Scoop, Scandal and Strife: A Study of Photography in Newspapers.* London: Lund Humphries.

Jay, Martin. 1988. "Scopic Regimes of Modernity." In *Vision and Visuality,* edited by Hal Foster. Seattle: Bay Press.

Keinan, Giora, Avi Sadeh, and Sefi Rosen. 2003. "Attitudes and Reactions to Media Coverage of Terrorist Acts." *Journal of Community Sociology* 31, no. 2: 149–65.

López Mondéjar, Publio. 1997. *Historia de la fotografía en España.* Barcelona: Lunwerg.

Lowe, Donald M. 1982. *History of Bourgeois Perception.* Chicago: University of Chicago Press.

Parejo, Nekane. 2004. *Fotografía y muerte: Representación gráfica de los atentados de ETA (1968–1977).* Leioa: Servicio Editorial de la Universidad del País Vasco.

Reinares, Fernando. 1993. "Características y formas del terrorismo político en las sociedades industriales avanzadas." *Revista Internacional de Sociología* 5 (May–August): 35–67.

Schmid, Alex P. 1989. "Terrorism and the Media: The Ethics of Publicity." *Terrorism and Political Violence* 1, no. 4 (October): 539–65.

Sontag, Susan. 1977. *On Photography.* New York: Farrar, Straus and Giroux.

8

The Basque Press and Terrorism, 1990–2009: From Telling the Facts to Complicity against ETA

José Ignacio Armentia and José María Caminos

Translated by Jennifer Martin

ETA's armed activity has occupied an important space in the Basque Country and Spanish press. The first deadly attack that this organization claimed took place on June 7, 1968. The victim was José Ángel Pardines, a civil guard. However, authors such as Rogelio Alonso, Florencio Domínguez, and Marcos García Rey (2010) suggested that the first death caused by this terrorist group was that of Begoña Urroz Ibarrola, twenty-two months of age, killed by a bomb explosion in the Amara railway station in Donostia-San Sebastián, which occurred on June 27, 1960. Ernest Lluch pointed out that hypothesis in a press article published in 2000. Nevertheless, other authors such as historian Iñaki Egaña (2010) disagreed with this point of view and attributed the Amara attack to the Directorio Revolucionario Ibérico de Liberación (Iberian Revolutionary Liberation Directorate, or DRIL), a Franco opposition group that was responsible for several attacks between 1960 and 1964.

* This text is based on research financed by the Spanish Ministry of Science and Innovation, entitled *The Evolution in the Coverage of Violent Deaths in the Basque Country Press* (Reference: CSO2010-19855).

According to the data provided on the Spanish Ministry of the Interior's website, ETA killed forty-four people between 1968 and November of 1975 (the time of Franco's death). Between that date and December 2009, the reported number of casualties caused by this group was 784.[1]

The ETA attacks particularly intensified at the end of the 1970s, reaching their peak in 1980, the year in which ninety-two people were killed. It was only in 1989 that the number of victims dropped to below twenty, and that was most likely due to the truce upheld by the organization for the talks in Algiers with the PSOE (Partido Socialista Obrero Español, Spanish Socialist Worker's Party) government during the first quarter of that year.

It was during the 1990s when a decrease in ETA's deadly activity in relation to the previous years was seen. The truce decreed between September 1988 and November 1999, during which talks took place with the government of José María Aznar, probably explains why 1999 was the first year in Spain without deaths from terrorism since 1971.

The breaking of that cease-fire caused a new upturn in ETA's activity in 2000, with twenty-three deaths. However, from 2001 onward, the number of victims fell dramatically, and there were even three years (2004, 2005, and 2008) in which no new killings were recorded. It should be noted that the new truce maintained by ETA between March 22 and December 29 of 2006 was preceded by a period of more than two years without deadly attacks. The armed organization also held a cease-fire between September 1998 and November 28, 1999.

The repeated police successes in the fight against ETA in the past decade and the collaboration of the French state in the persecution of the organization's members were, without a doubt, factors that also explained the important decrease in the number of terrorist attacks.

As we will see in the following analysis, the number of casualties caused by ETA has not always been in parallel with the media coverage. Even though the number of deaths stood at similar levels in 1990 and in 2000 (twenty-five and twenty-three, respectively), over ten years an expo-

---

1. In the list of ETA victims collected by the Ministry of the Interior, those claimed by the Comandos Autónomos Anticapitalistas (Autonomous Anticapitalist Commandos), an armed group whose origin could be traced to a split that occurred in ETA pm (political-military) in 1976, were also included. The Comandos Autónomos (Autonomous Commandos) were responsible for several attacks between 1978 and 1984, causing the death of twenty-seven people; among them was Senator Enrique Casas of the PSE-PSOE.

nential increase took place in the attention that the media dedicated to terrorist actions—attention that was continued in 2009.

Sample Selection

For the study on the evolution of the Basque press coverage of deadly ETA attacks, the killings that occurred during 1990 (twenty-five), 2000 (twenty-three), and 2009 (three) have been taken into account in the *El Correo Español, Deia, Egin-Gara,* and *El País* newspapers.

The first three are published in the Basque Country, whereas *El País* is the best-selling newspaper in Spain and also has an edition specifically for the Basque Country, which is produced in its regional office in Bilbao.

El Correo is published in Bilbao and belongs to Grupo Vocente, which has a total of thirteen newspapers (*El Diario Vasco,* published in Donostia-San Sebastián, is among them) that are mainly provincial in scope, except for the national *ABC. El Correo* is a center-right newspaper, monarchist and critical of Basque nationalism, but it is a proponent of the Basque Statue of Autonomy, as well as of the Spanish Constitution. This paper was founded in 1910 under the name *El Pueblo Vasco,* although during the Spanish Civil War it was forced to merge with a Falangist publication called *El Correo Español.* The result of this merger was the adoption of the name *El Correo Español–El Pueblo Vasco* in 1938. In 2009 this publication had, according to the OJD,[2] a circulation of 110,826 copies, which made it the seventh best-selling general interest newspaper in Spain. According to EGM,[3] *El Correo* had 503,000 readers in the aforementioned year.

Table 8.1. Circulation Figures of the Analyzed Media

Newspapers	1990	2000	2009
El Correo	130,032	132,113	110,826
Deia	48,313	n/d*	19,087
Egin/Gara	44,264	52,311**	n/d**
El País	375,875	436,302	391,815

Source: OJD.
Deia was not found in OJD's documents for 2000.
**Egin* was closed in 1998, so the figure corresponded to OJD data from 1997. *Gara* was not found in this organization's audits.

---

2. The Circulation Audit Office (La Organización para la Justificación de la Difusión, OJD) is the organism that monitors the sales of Spanish press.

3. The General Media Study (Estudio General de Medios, EGM) monitors the audience of different communication mediums using a survey method.

Table 8.2. Audience (in thousands of readers)

Newspapers	1990	2000	2009
El Correo	505	591	503
Deia	118	109	87
Egin/Gara	126	142	92*
El País	1.452	1.447	2.081

Source: EGM.

*Data correspond to 2008. *Gara* was not found in the 2009 survey.

Deia was founded in Bilbao in 1977 and has always been viewed as a newspaper that agrees with the postulates of the Basque Nationalist Party (EAJ-PNV by its Basque and Spanish acronyms), a moderate political party, though with a pro-Basque sovereignty ideology, and against ETA's armed activity. The EAJ-PNV held the Basque government presidency nonstop from 1979 until 2009. Patxi López of the PSE-PSOE (the Socialist Party of the Basque Country by its Spanish acronym), with the support of the People's Party (PP by its Spanish acronym), was elected as the *lehendakari* (Basque president) on May 5, 2009.

Deia presently belongs to Grupo Noticias, which publishes three other newspapers in Euskadi and in Navarra. According to OJD, *Deia* had a circulation of 19,087 copies in 2009. Its audience, according to EGM, totaled 87,000 readers.

Egin was also founded in 1977, in Hernani (Gipuzkoa), and its ideological orientation has been identified with the most radical form of Basque nationalism. This newspaper's alleged affinity with ETA caused judge Baltasar Garzón to order its closure in June 1998. In 1999 *Gara*, a publication holding the same ideology and that, in great part, was staffed with journalists from the discontinued newspaper, occupied its space. *Gara* did not appear in the OJD audits. In 2008,[4] the EGM estimated this newspaper's readership to be 92,000.

El País was founded in Madrid in 1976 and quickly became the best-selling newspaper in Spain. The innovations developed in both its content and in its design, as well as its newsstand success, turned this paper into the model for many other publications to follow. It is the main publication of Grupo Prisa and is distributed throughout Spain. This leading newspaper has had a specific edition for Euskadi since 1997. The editorial

---

4. *Gara* was not found in the EGM data corresponding to 2009.

line of *El País* is center-left and is politically close to the PSOE. In 2009 this paper reached a circulation of 391,815 copies (the highest selling in Spain) and had a readership of 2,081,000 people.

Information Policies

The media reports on given subjects, complying with standards that are modified over time. That is why, in 1990, the reporting of the ETA attacks had little to do with the strategies used twenty years later by the same media.

Since PSOE's rise to power in 1982, the different governments of Spain and the Basque Country have sought to reach a consensus on a common information policy regarding terrorist attacks and ETA.

Initially, at the end of the seventies, the idea that the media should attempt to silence the ETA attacks emerged from the political sphere. Some well-known journalists and media bosses shared this initiative. However, the belief that concealing information about terrorist acts did not contribute to anything positive ultimately prevailed. On the contrary, it could create a greater expectation of those actions. It should be noted that Spain emerged from a dictatorship in which silence on the part of the media never managed to quell political or social demands, nor the ETA attacks and their consequences.

Media silence was rejected because it only helped to relegate the citizens' right to information in a free society to the background. The information policy that the news media was supposed to adhere to in the face of terrorist attacks was a different matter. Arcadi Espada (2002) shared this point of view when he affirmed, "Journalists are made to give an account of our times. And obviously, in this account of our times, in that distorted mirror, or not, by the side of the road, violence, rage, madness, irrationalism, crime, and the death penalty all deserve their place in the end. That is why, because evil exists in life, I firmly believe that it must be in the media."

It was true that one of the purposes of the terrorist acts was to get exposure, but it would be overly simplistic to think that that was ETA's only objective. Publication was important, of course, but it was merely a part of the multilateral effects that the armed actions sought. The terrorist attacks had a highly propagandistic component, not just directed at the media but also at their social, political, and vindictive environment—toward their prisoners and their members. That is, dissemination was just part of their objectives. Terrorism was not primarily an act of communication. Just as Miquel Rodrigo Alsina (1991, 32) pointed out: "Acknowledging an important, but not decisive, communicative dimension of terrorism is another very different matter. Terrorist acts are events that fall within a communication system whose production logic will turn them into news."

Since the media silence idea was rejected and the terrorist acts had an important communicative component, the political arena encouraged the media to maintain a common information policy regarding the attacks. However, these recommendations were not immediately reflected in the media, and discrepancies even appeared within them over how to journalistically treat the ETA attacks.

The first attempts to homogenize the media's information policy concerning terrorism arose in 1983 while the PSOE governed in Spain. Born under the presidency of Felipe González,[5] the ZEN (Spanish acronym for Special Northern Zone) Plan considered, among other things, the possibility of launching an offensive media policy against the terrorist attacks. The following were among the plan's proposals: make efforts to ensure that ETA appears as little as possible in the media; focus all policy interventions on the peace and well-being of the people and not on terrorism; provide periodic information through third parties (daily or weekly newspapers); and advance information about conflicts among terrorists, their unusual ideologies, their business dealings, and their criticizable customs. It was sufficient for the information to be credible in order for it to be exploited. However, these recommendations would not see their effects until a decade later.

In 1985, the Basque Parliament passed a decalogue to more effectively fight ETA. The eighth point required that, while respecting freedom of expression, media bosses collaborate with institutions representative of the popular will and through the media, within their scope, develop "the social atmosphere necessary for spreading the values of mutual respect, tolerance, and the rejection of violence and terrorism."

These instructions materialized in a pact, known as the Ajuria Enea Pact,[6] promoted by the Basque government in 1988, in which the men-

---

5. On October 7, 1983, the Basque Parliament discussed the ZEN Plan and the amendments that the Basque parliamentary groups presented to them. The plan and the discussion that took place in the Basque Chamber can be viewed at www.archive.org/details/PnvPlanZen.

6. The full text of the Ajuria Enea Pact can be read at www.filosofía.org/his/h1988ae.htm.

tion of the importance of the media in the fight against terrorism was extended to the role that should be played by educators, who were also viewed as decisive protagonists in the pacification process due to their influence over social behavior.

It was not until after 1997, specifically after the July 13 assassination of Miguel Ángel Blanco, a councilman for the PP in Ermua, when an important change was observed in the media's coverage of ETA attacks. Arcadi Espada (2002) confirmed the change adopted by the media after this attack: "Until the death of Miguel Ángel Blanco, which made a deep impact, terrorism and its victims had been minimized, and the murderers actively and passively mythicized. And I'm making nothing up in saying this. This is the result of an analysis from the newspapers at that time."

Any attack, by its very essence, meets the specific requirements of a newsworthy event. An attack involves the violent rupture of the normal course of things. It is an unforeseen event, not probable, and does away with the media's production routines. An attack is marked by such expediency that it requires intensive and quick work from the media in order to report the unexpected attack. A news story, despite being responsive and limited to a very short time period, carries pieces of information on many occasions that are of great interest: political and social statements, mobilization calls, and so on. Therefore, terrorist attacks more than meet the requirements of being newsworthy events.

In the late 1990s, the media developed the awareness that they could play an essential role in the fight against terrorism and that coverage of terrorist acts did not have to be neutral. From that decade and on into 2000, the media were clearly aware that reports on terrorism had to be an effective instrument for fighting against such activity.

Margarita Robles, a member of the General Council of the Judiciary, emphasized the importance of the media's role in both the search for conflict solutions as well as in the reporting of those conflicts: "And it is because of that, that importance of the media, that all of the political powers in all countries and at all times, have had a particular interest in controlling the media or else in building excellent relationships with them" (Peñalva 2000, 27).

Authors such as Petxo Idoyaga and Txema Ramírez de la Piscina (2000, 273) spoke of the media's active role against terrorism between the years of 1998 and 2000: "Cayetano González Hermosilla, Communication Manager at the Ministry of the Interior, recently highlighted the 'maturity' demonstrated by the media across the entire State in addressing what is called the 'problem of terrorism' while he stressed the need to banish the idea of journalistic neutrality when reporting on these issues."

This belligerent policy against terrorism was already so rooted that in January 2001, Alberto Ruíz-Gallardón, leader of the PP and then president of the Community of Madrid (Comunidad de Madrid), removed the general director of Madrid's regional television channel, Telemadrid, because he thought that a report on the situation in the Basque Country broadcast by that public entity was not adverse to ETA terrorism.

In January 2002, the board of directors of the Ente Público Radiotelevisón Española (RTVE Public Entity) prepared a document on terrorism coverage in which the following was asserted:

> In a system of full democratic freedoms, terrorist activities should be the object of rigorous coverage and free from any type of concessions and speculation. It is up to the media, its leaders, and its professionals to establish appropriate self-monitoring of information, particularly in the case of a clash between the freedoms and rights of citizens to be informed and respect for judicial proceedings and policies that the legal system requires. (RTVE Administrative Board 2002)

The media was now aware that the journalistic treatment of terrorism could not be neutral. According to the RTVE document, neutrality could turn into complicity when the essential principles of democracy were at stake.

Throughout the past decade the media explored an active information policy against terrorism in depth. Some texts contextualized the information that was given about the attacks: the horror that was caused, the responsibility of those that committed the acts, the consequences of the violence, and so on.

For that purpose, they also formed a specific language to describe the violent acts. Hence the recommendation that RTVE made for its journalists to try to eliminate from their daily use , although in quotation marks, certain terms that had a propagandistic element: "executed," "people's jails," "revolutionary tax," "information and support commands," and even the use of an "alias" that sought to create an air of familiarity with the terrorists (Consejo de Administración de RTVE 2002). It was ultimately about using a vocabulary that prevented the justification and dignification of terrorist activity.

El Correo: 1990, 2000, 2009

El Correo was one of the newspapers in which the evolution in addressing the deadly ETA attacks during the three analyzed time periods was more prominent. Perhaps the most striking change was found in the front-page headlines.

Front-Page Analysis

In 1990, *El Correo* published all of the recent deadly attacks by ETA on its front pages, but 14.3 percent of the time the subject matter was treated as secondary. In 2000, however, all the attacks carried out were front-page news, an information policy that was still maintained as of 2009.

As far as the use of graphic material on the front page, if in 1990 photos were published on the front page in a little more than in half of the cases, in 2000 they were published in almost all of the attacks. This trend continued until 2009. That year's front pages featured full-page photos.

In 1990, the photos that were published always showed the damages caused by the attacks; they never emphasized the human aspect. This trend made an important turnaround, and in 2000 half of the published photos showed the damages caused by the attacks, but the other half captured human aspects.

The type of headline that *El Correo* used to describe the attacks was also significant. In 100 percent of the cases in 1990, the headline was informative and free of any journalistic interpretation. However, in 2000, a change toward more interpretive headlines began. So, 77.7 percent of the headlines were merely informative, while 22.2 percent were interpretive. This change in headlines was more extensive in 2009, and appellative-opinionated headlines were used for the three attacks that occurred that year (100 percent). That is, the headlines included opinions.

Informative Texts Study

In 1990 *El Correo* published an average of 1.1 pages per attack, which was not a large, informative spread. A significant increase in the number of pages occurred in 2000, reaching an average of 8.7 pages per attack. This continued to progressively increase until arriving at 17 pages published per attack in 2009.

With regards to the type of story written about the attacks, it was mainly informative in 1990, although background information also began to be published about the ETA commandos responsible for the attacks and a few biographical sketches of those assassinated were written. In 2000, we saw a proliferation of contextual information, biographical sketches of victims, information about their friends, people close to them, neighbors of the sites where the stories unfolded, as well as information and declarations from the victims' relatives. This trend to "humanize" the attacks was maintained and strengthened over the years, and along the same line, a wide range of texts were published in 2009 that aided in examining and contextualizing the attacks.

Graphic Material Study

El Correo published a total of 20 photographs of the attacks on its inner pages in 1990, which left a percentage of 1.4 photos per day. However, a qualitative jump in the use of this graphic material was made in 2000. *El Correo* published a total of 229 photographs on its inner pages, which meant an average of 12.7 photos per attack. The number of photos increased even more in 2009, reaching an average of 21, an extremely high figure that was well above the trend set ten years before.

Regarding the type of pictures used, in 1990 *El Correo* favored photographs that captured the victims and the damage caused by the attacks (85 percent) over photos that were on a more strictly human scale (15 percent). An important turnaround concerning the type of photos used also occurred in 2000. Photographs with an obvious human angle were mainly published (65 percent) before strictly contextual, political photos (23 percent) and photos of the damage caused (11.8 percent). Photos of people occupied a relevant place in 2009 (45.2 percent), followed by contextual photos (38.1 percent), and finally, photos of the damage caused by the attacks (16.6 percent).

The publication of infographics also became more widespread. They were used on three occasions (21.4 percent) in 1990 as an important resource to explain the ETA attacks. However, in 2000, infographics appeared in 88.8 percent of the articles; only 11.2 percent did not use them. Their use was consolidated in 2009 when 100 percent of the cases used them.

Opinion Analysis

In 1990, *El Correo* acknowledged editorials concerning ETA attacks on its front page in only 14.2 percent of the cases. In addition, it printed opinion pieces at the rate of 21.4 percent, with an average of 1.3 opinion pieces.

In 100 percent of the cases during the year 2000, the front page of *El Correo* called attention to the existence of editorials dedicated to ETA attacks. Furthermore, the editorials began on the front page 66.6 percent of the time, either through a headline or by means of a headline and a couple of paragraphs. Additionally, in 50 percent of the cases, it published opinion pieces with an average of 1.8 articles per attack.

Also in 2009, in 100 percent of the cases, the front page of *El Correo* announced the existence of editorials on ETA attacks, although the editorial itself did not begin on the same page in either of the three occasions. Opinion pieces on the attacks appeared in 100 percent of the cases. That was due to an information policy that this newspaper had consolidated over the years. An average of five opinion pieces per attack were published.

Deia: 1990, 2000, 2009

Deia went from devoting an average of 0.99 pages per day to the deadly ETA attacks in 1990 to an average of 11.4 pages in 2000, which shows the change that occurred in the coverage of that type of news. *Deia* is a daily newspaper with a moderate Basque nationalism editorial line and has been critical of ETA violence.

Front-Page Analysis

In the period between 1990 and 2000, *Deia* went from giving preferential attention to the deadly attacks caused by ETA to giving them absolute priority. It should be noted that during 1990 there had been four events that this newspaper's bosses thought were more newsworthy than the ETA killings: declarations from Xabier Arzalluz, the EAJ-PNV president at the time, on the Statute of Autonomy; the Kilometroak celebration or the Basque-language-schools (*ikastolas*) festival in Gipuzkoa; the suicide in Paris of a judge involved in the fight against terrorism; and the resignation of Bilbao's mayor, José María Gorordo.

Another aspect in which the newspaper's evolution on the coverage of ETA's attacks was evident was the number of pages that were dedicated to such news. Thus it went from an average of 1 page per day in 1990 to 11.4 pages in 2000. The figure decreased slightly in 2009, to 9.5 pages per day.

Graphic changes were also evident on the front page. It should be noted that twenty years ago the technical limitations of the time were a serious obstacle to printing images from events that occurred at the last minute. That most likely explained the reason why a third of news reports on the attacks lacked photos in 1990. By contrast, in the year 2000, there were only three occasions in which the front page did not carry photos along with these reports. Furthermore, the change that occurred in the content of these photos was significant. Unlike what happened in 1990, photos that captured the consequences of the attacks were not exclusively used anymore in 2000, but images with human content also appeared (for example, photos of the victim's family) that came to make up a third of the total number published.

Headlines did not escape the change in the media's coverage of these events either. In 1990, they were all strictly informative. In 2000, headlines were much more interpretive, when they weren't opinionated. In fact, for the final murders that occurred that year, *Deia* included "but ETA does not listen" as a teaser (or kicker) on the front page.

Informative Texts Study

From 1990 to 2000, there was an exponential increase in the space that *Deia* gave to the deadly ETA attacks. It went from less than fifteen pages, to no fewer than 206. It could be said that these acts were converted into an informative event of crucial importance for the Bilbao newspaper. In fact, the average number of pages per day went from 0.99 in 1990 to 11.4 in 2000—a trend that still continued (although with a slight decrease) in 2009.

Along with the increase in space, an increase in the variety of the texts used also occurred. In 1990, 78.9 percent of the published material corresponded to informative articles about the attack. Only 7.8 percent of the texts could place themselves in that category in 2000. This meant that the attacks were addressed from points of view that differed from the simple reporting of the facts. Biographical sketches of the victims, contextual information, and above all the reactions of the political parties and institutions were frequently used. These last two details amounted to approximately half of the texts published in 2000.

Graphic Material Study

In 1990, *Deia* published twenty-three photos of deadly ETA attacks on its inner pages. This offered readers an average of 1.5 photos per day. Of these images, 87 percent captured the consequences of the attack (e.g., the victim's body, the twisted iron mess from a car bomb, etc.). The remaining 13 percent showed a more human type of content, mainly including the relatives or peers of those killed. During this year, *Deia* did not publish a single infographic on these subject matters. In this regard, it should be noted that the infographic boom began in Spain during the Gulf War in January of 1991, and that prior to that conflict the use infographics was rather limited.

In 2000, the number of photographs amounted to 460, with an average of 25.5 daily images. The great innovation with regard to 1990, in addition to the evident quantitive increase, was the abundant use of contextual photos (67.1 percent of the total), mostly of politicians, with which the media sought to illustrate the approvals and condemnations they made. It was also significant that the number of photographs with human content surpassed that of explicit images of the attacks. During this year, the use of infographics was fully consolidated. On a third of the occasions, this method was employed to graphically explain how the attacks had been carried out.

In 2009 the average number of photos per day amounted to 15.5. A predominance of contextual-type images (51.6 percent) was also observed during that year. Furthermore, pictures with human content doubled in number (32 percent) compared to those that displayed effects of the attack. The use of infographics became somewhat standard, as they were the resource used in the three deadly attacks of that year.

Opinion Analysis

In 1990 *Deia* offered a fundamentally informative focus on the attacks. In fact, it had never published editorials or opinion pieces related to these on its front page before. Its inner pages maintained the same trend and the news articles were not accompanied by opinion pieces.

This outlook changed completely in 2000. The newspaper included the title of its editorial on the front page for the deadly attacks that occurred during that year, with the exception of one. Also, the presence of opinion pieces along with the informational articles became the norm. This occurred in 66 percent of the cases. The average number of opinion pieces was 2.7.

In 2009, although editorial pieces were devoted to both ETA attacks, they did not begin on the front page. The number of opinion pieces also decreased. There was only one, which suggested a significant decrease in comparison with the previous analyzed year.

Egin-Gara: **1990, 2000, 2009**

As noted earlier, *Egin* was closed in July 1998 by the magistrate of the National Court, Baltasar Garzón, as part of Case No. 18/98 because it was thought that *Egin* formed part of the ETA "network." The newspaper *Gara*, founded on January 30, 1999, whose staff mainly came from *Egin*, occupied its ideological space.

Front-Page Analysis

The change that was produced on the front pages of *Gara* in 2000 regarding what happened at *Egin* in 1990 was especially significant. This last paper only featured the fatal ETA attacks on its front page in 46.6 percent of the occasions. *Gara* featured 94.4 percent of the attacks on the front page; that is, the importance given to these events doubled, a trend that was upheld in 2009.

The front-page headlines of both *Egin* and *Gara* clearly took an informative angle, although some changes were also seen in this case. While all of *Egin*'s front-page headlines were informative, a third of *Gara*'s headlines in 2000 were informative-interpretive, a trend that reached 50 percent in 2009. Nonetheless, opinion pieces did not materialize in any of the three time periods.

More than half of *Egin*'s front pages concerning the ETA attacks lacked photographs. In 2000, *Gara* lacked images only 16.6 percent of the time. Photographs were present in all of the cases studied in 2009. The images always displayed the effects of the attack. Photos of the people affected were never placed on the front page.

Informative Texts Study

Neither *Egin* nor *Gara* had been characterized by conceding excessive space on its inner pages to the ETA killings. *Egin* devoted two-thirds of a page to each one of those events in 1990. Ten years later, *Gara* devoted an average of 3.7 pages to these incidents, practically the same proportion that was observed in 2009.

Just as what was seen with the analyzed text from other papers, an evolution in the type of texts used on the inner pages of these newspapers was also observed.

Egin almost exclusively published informative articles on the attacks (87.5 percent). *Gara* granted significant space in 2000 to politicians' reactions (28.5 percent of articles) and to the reactions of institutional representatives (33.5 percent). However, there were hardly any texts that reported on the victims' neighborhood environment (0.7 percent) or the reactions of the victims' families (1.5 percent).

A more informative policy returned to a certain extent in 2009. Still, the number of texts on the political parties' reactions matched those related to the account of the attacks.

Graphic Material Study

Egin published a total of 17 photos of the attacks in 1990, for an average 1.13 per day. Except for one of the human images, the rest dealt with the attacks' consequences (e.g., death, destruction, etc.).

Gara notably increased the number of photos it used in 2000. It published 86, an average of 4.7 per day. Of those, 29 percent captured images of the attack. Another 62 percent could be categorized as contextual, since politicians, institutional representatives, and other government officials appeared in them. The remaining 8.1 percent corresponded to human content photos.

The average number of photos per day (4.5) was maintained in 2009, although the percentage of contextual photos shot up to 78 percent. Those relating to the consequences of the attacks and those classified as human were equally divided in the remaining percentage.

Furthermore, the employment of infographics was anecdotal in 1990, since *Egin* only utilized this resource on one occasion. The situation was very different in 2000. *Gara* published infographic material in 83 percent of the attacks. This exhaustive use of explanatory graphics continued in 2009, given that this material appeared in the three analyzed days.

Opinion Analysis

Neither *Egin* nor *Gara* were characterized by including opinion pieces on their pages devoted to ETA's deadly attacks. Nevertheless, while *Egin* did not make any reference on its front page to editorials on the attacks, *Gara* announced the existence of an editorial on its front page in 66 percent of the occasions in 2000. In 2009 reference was made of an editorial on the front page for only one of the three attacks, while the trend of not including opinions on the inner pages was maintained.

El País: 1990, 2000, 2009

Although *El País* is published in Madrid, it has also had a specific Euskadi edition produced in Bilbao since 1997 and has always paid preferential attention to Basque politics as well as to ETA activity.

Front-Page Analysis

Throughout 1990 *El País* maintained an information policy that could be called "second rate" when it came time to report on ETA attacks. The attacks were considered to be the day's most important subject in only 21.4 percent of the cases, placed second in 28.4 percent of the cases, and were a third-tier subject 42.8 percent of the time. We understand third-tier information to be that which makes up a column, front-page calls (small, single headlines), or brief texts placed at the bottom of the front page.

When the newspaper *El País* placed the attacks at a second or third tier of priority, it chose to stress matters of international politics, national politics, and the Spanish economy above them. However, the eighteen deadly ETA attacks that occurred in 2000 appeared on the *El País* front page, and more significantly, the event was the main story on its front page every time, thus breaking with the information policy of ten years prior. This trend was maintained until 2009; two attacks that occurred that year were prominently published on the front page.

Regarding graphic material, in 1990 *El País* did not publish photographs of the attacks on its front page in 64.2 percent of the cases. Furthermore, when it did publish photos, they all consisted of the damage caused by the attacks; none of them highlighted more human elements (e.g., victims, relatives, friends, neighbors, etc.). In 2000 however, photographs were used to illustrate 88.8 percent of the attacks, and images that carried clear human components began to be published, detailing the pain of the attacks, and of the victims' family and friends. That same trend continued with the graphic material used in 2009.

With regard to front-page headlines, 92.8 percent were informative in 1990, and there was only one occasion (7.1 percent) in which a small interpretation was introduced instead. In 2000 *El País* decided to explore the interpretive trend, and 33.3 percent of its front-page headlines included journalistic interpretations. This trend was gradually consolidated, and in 2009, 100 percent of the headlines were interpretive.

Informative Texts Study

Over the fourteen days analyzed in 1990 *El País* published an average of 0.6 pages per attack; that is, it did not view the attacks as subject matter of great informative relevance. In 2000, however, a qualitative jump was made when the paper published an average of 7.4 pages per attack, which represented a fundamental turning point with regard to what was being published ten years before. This trend suffered a considerable drop, and in 2009 an average of only three pages was given per attack.

With respect to the type of coverage on these pages, *El País* turned to the use of an informative description of the attacks in 1990. It included some contextual information on the ETA commandos, other possible attacks, and so on in only 21.4 percent of the cases, and included biographical sketches of the people killed in 14.2 percent of the cases. A whole set of journalistic elements began to unfold in 2009.

Biographical sketches of those killed appeared in 72.2 percent of the attack-site coverage, statements from neighbors were included in 44.4 percent, and statements from relatives were in 27.7 percent. The pages were concluded with condemnations from parties, syndicates, civil organizations, celebrities, the church, and so on.

That informative trend continued in 2009 since coverage included contextual material, short biographies of victims, environmental information, interviews with family and friends, and so forth in 100 percent of the cases during that year.

Graphic Material Study

El País published a total of 12 photographs of the attacks on its inner pages in 1990, which was a percentage of 0.8 photos per day. That is, there were days in which this newspaper did not publish any photo on its inner pages. Important changes were made in 2000 when the percentage of photos published per attack was 7.3, but that average dropped down to 3 daily photos in 2009.

Regarding the type of photos published, all of them (100 percent) addressed the victims and the damages caused by the attacks. A change occurred in this theme in 2000: photos of the attacks represented 19 percent, while photos with a human component, reflecting people in the middle of the tragedy, appeared 48 percent of the time and contextual photos of political statements and the like rose to 32.8 percent. In 2009, contextual photos declined compared to the ten previous years (16.6 percent), photos of the attacks grew (33.3 percent), and those of a human component were notably solidified (50 percent).

The emergence of infographics to better illustrate the attacks was another relevant aspect regarding graphic material. While in 1990 *El País* did not use infographics to better explain the reports, in 2000 the newspaper published informational drawings in 83.3 percent of the occasions. This trend solidified until 2009 when infographic material was used to illustrate the three deadly attacks that occurred that year.

Opinion Analysis

In 1990 the front page of *El País* did not, on any occasion, report the existence of editorials devoted to the ETA attacks and did not publish any opinion piece in its pages regarding those attacks.

However, a notice of an editorial concerning the subject appeared on the front page in 94.4 percent of the cases in 2000. Furthermore, in 16.6 percent of the cases, the editorials themselves began on the front page and continued on the opinion pages. In these cases the beginning may have been just a headline or several paragraphs. *El País* thus succeeded in giving opinion pieces greater importance. *El País* announced the editorials concerning the ETA attacks on its front page on both of the days analyzed (100 percent) in 2009. In addition, on one occasion the editorial began on the front page itself and was continued on the opinion pages.

El País also began to publish opinion articles in 2009, contrary to what was published in 1990. On seven days, in 38.8 percent of the attacks, *El País* published twenty-one opinion pieces on its inner pages, which represented a total of three per each of the seven days.

However, opinion articles regarding the attacks did not appear on either of the three days analyzed in 2009. This was due to the newspaper's inability to consolidate an information policy over the years.

Conclusions

During the first few years of the policy transition, the media rejected the silence proposed by the government concerning the ETA attacks, and for many years they simply reported their acts without taking a clear common stand against terrorism. The imminence of the Franco dictatorship with its permanent media silence and the political strength of the organizations from ETA's environment were not unconnected to the information policy that rejected the silence.

The attempts of the media to reach a consensus on an information policy to fight terrorism did not take shape until the 1990s. A profound change took place between 1990 and 2000 in the press's coverage of deadly ETA attacks. The reaction of the people and the media to the June 1997 kidnapping and assassination of Miguel Ángel Blanco, a PP councilman in Ermua (Bizkaia), could be seen as a turning point in the role that the press would play in reporting on terrorism.

It could be said that when the year 2000 arrived, the media were aware of their role in the fight against terrorism and they had become an active instrument in combating it. Most of the Basque press had ceased being a mere vehicle that reported on ETA attacks with the greatest sterility possible. This informative trend was still maintained in 2009, but not as significantly as in 2000, perhaps because of the drastic reduction in deadly ETA activity.

This change in the media's attitude over the years was reflected in a gradual and considerable increase in the number of pages that were devoted to the attacks, as well as in the increased space given to them on the front pages. The front-page headlines on the attacks also underwent a significant change: interpretive titling replaced the merely informative over the years. *El Correo* stood out in regard to this tendency by publishing headlines with clear opinionative components in 2009.

The increased press involvement in the condemnation of ETA was also observed in the graphic material used. The number of images used gradually increased. In addition to the appearance of photographs showing the havoc caused by the attacks, over the years images with human content were introduced that were charged with emotion (e.g., relatives of the victims crying, friends, neighbors, work associates).

Regarding the formal presentation of information on the attacks, mention must be made of the irruption of infographics as the fundamental visual to explain the development of the events that occurred to the reader.

The media's editorial policy in the face of terrorism also underwent important changes. In 1990, the media used its front pages to mention the existence of editorials on just a few occasions. In 2000, however, editorial announcements about the ETA attacks almost always appeared on the front pages, and even began on the front pages. Opinion articles and columns underwent a similar evolution, and although they were not common in 1990, they were clearly established in 2000 and continued until

2009 with their corresponding ups and downs. Opinions condemning the ETA attacks were frequently found during this past decade.

References

Alonso, Rogelio, Florencio Domínguez, and Marcos García Rey. 2010. *Vidas rotas: La historia de los hombres, las mujeres y los niños víctimas de ETA*. Madrid: Espasa.

Consejo de Administración de RTVE. 2002. *Documento sobre tratamiento informativo del terrorismo*. Madrid (January 15).

Egaña, Iñaki. 2010. "Cómo se construye una mentira." *Gara*, February 12.

Espada, Arcadi. 2002. "Diarios: El tratamiento periodístico del terrorismo." Lecture for *El Correo-Aula de Cultura Virtual*. Accessed January 17, 2012. http://servicios.elcorreo.com/auladecultura/arcadiespada1.html.

Idoyaga, Petxo, and Txema Ramírez de la Piscina. 2000. "Política informativa de *El País* y *ABC* ante la nueva situación política del País Vasco (1998–2000)." *Zer: Revista de Estudios de Comunicación* 10: 257–79.

Lluch, Ernest. 2000. "La primera víctima de ETA." *El Diario Vasco*, September 19.

Pacto de Ajuria Enea. Accessed January 17, 2012. www.filosofía.org/his/h1988ae.htm.

Peñalva, José Luis, ed. 2000. *Medios de Comunicación y Procesos de Paz*. Leioa: Servicio Editorial de la Universidad del País Vasco.

Plan ZEN. Accessed January 17, 2012. www.archive.org/details/PnvPlanZen.

Rodrigo Alsina, Miquel. 1991. *Los medios de comunicación ante el terrorismo*. Barcelona: Icaria.

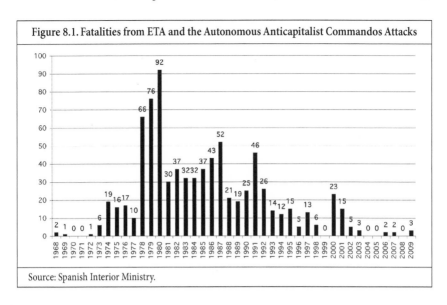

Figure 8.1. Fatalities from ETA and the Autonomous Anticapitalist Commandos Attacks

Source: Spanish Interior Ministry.

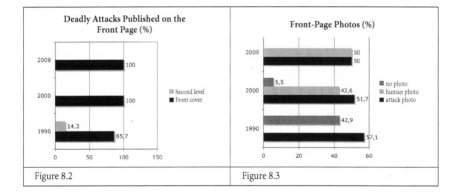

Figure 8.2

Figure 8.3

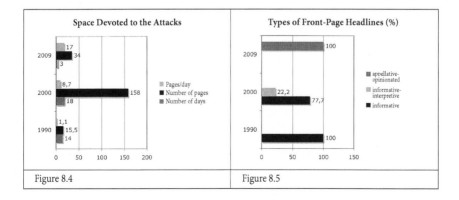

Figure 8.4

Figure 8.5

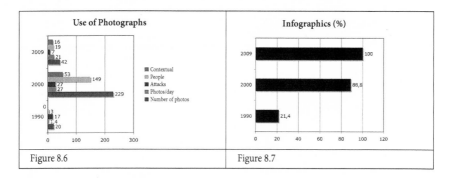

Figure 8.6

Figure 8.7

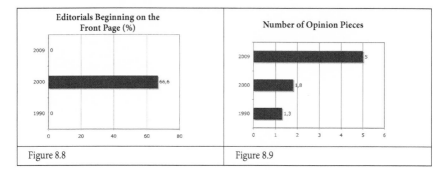

Figure 8.8

Figure 8.9

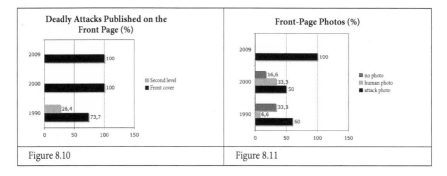

Figure 8.10

Figure 8.11

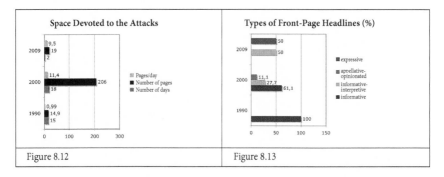

Figure 8.12

Figure 8.13

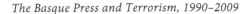

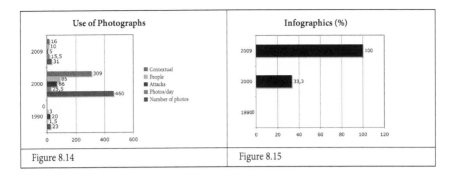

Figure 8.14

Figure 8.15

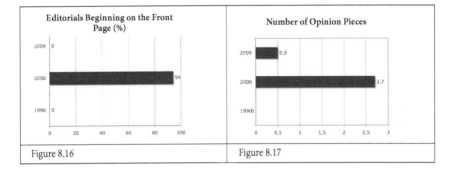

Figure 8.16

Figure 8.17

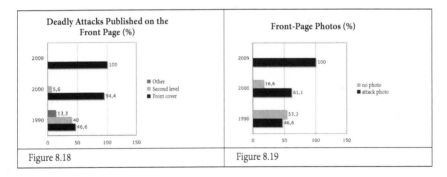

Figure 8.18

Figure 8.19

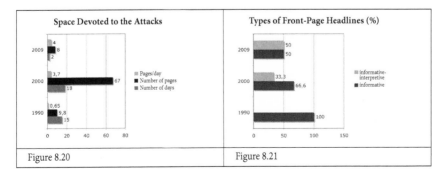

Figure 8.20

Figure 8.21

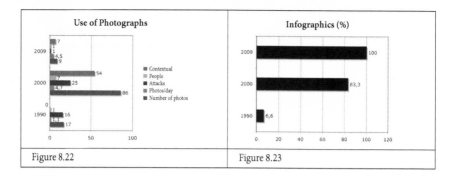

Figure 8.22

Figure 8.23

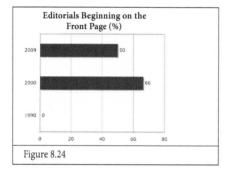

Figure 8.24

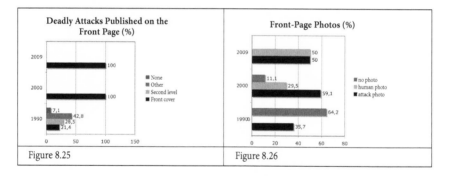

Figure 8.25

Figure 8.26

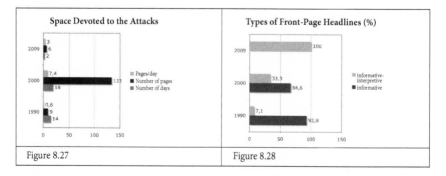

Figure 8.27

Figure 8.28

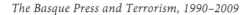

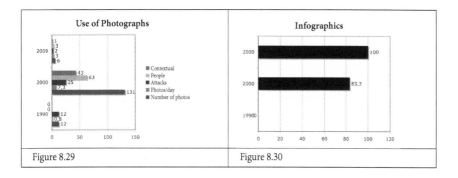

Figure 8.29

Figure 8.30

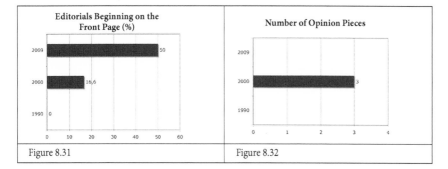

Figure 8.31

Figure 8.32

9

Humor, Violence, and Infotainment in the Basque Country: The *Vaya Semanita* Phenomenon on Basque Public Television, 2003–2005

Carmelo Moreno

Translated by Laura Bunt-MacRury

The aim of this chapter is to discuss a particular brand of humor in the first two seasons of the popular Basque comedy show *Vaya Semanita* (What a week), especially the episodes broadcasted on Euskal Telebista (ETB, Basque public television) from 2003 to 2005.[1] There is a simple reason for choosing this subject matter. For decades, political information in the Basque Country was governed by a habitual and acute seriousness, shaped by the experience of terrorism, violence, and extreme political polarization. Thus, it was difficult for the media to find humor of any kind in the form of political jokes or satire related to Basque politics in general, not to mention humor concerning issues of violence or terrorism. At present, however, the situation appears to be changing. Since 2003, the program *Vaya Semanita* has proved successful in the Basque region and in a certain ways has created a new conduit in mass media using political humor, especially when concerning the topics of political violence and terrorism.

This chapter is organized into three parts. The first part is theoretical and methodological in nature and seeks to elucidate the different theories given to the role of humor in modern societies in tandem with the hypoth-

---

1. The program is currently (2012) in its ninth season, 2011–2012.

esis and methodology that inform this study. The second part is a descriptive analysis that details the empirical outcome of the study. Finally, the third part summarizes the main conclusions and offers some reflection on the role of infotainment programs in addressing the phenomenon of violence.

Political Comedy: Comedic or Political?

"Infotainment" is a hybrid concept that refers to two types of activity: informing and entertaining—divergent notions that are increasingly fused. Supposedly, infotainment can mean two things. The first meaning refers to changes occurring in traditional serious formats for political information, such as news programs, which have sought to shape public opinion by introducing playful elements into information transmissions. The second meaning refers to the emergence of new ludic entertainment formats that handle political topics. That is, entertainment formats that "inform" on political matters in a pleasant, critical, or jovial manner, such as television series with political content, talk shows, commercials, videos, comedy shows, and chat shows (Baum 2003). In theory, the difference between the two is fundamental because a journalist who uses humor in a news program is not the same thing as a comedian who "reports" in the course of a comedy show. In practice, however, these distinctions are diminishing. Peter Sloterdijk explains that the emergence of infotainment in the mass media, even among those at ease with its usage, "is a phenomenon that reveals a shift in the media by means of passing on information through the generation of controversy via a provocative style of journalism and simplified mass hysteria" (2000, 88).

At the dawn of modernity, Thomas Hobbes, one of the first political theorists to analyze sociopolitical humor, warned that political humor is an extremely suspicious activity and should be treated with immense trepidation. This disposition, however, has changed from the time of the liberal bourgeois Enlightenment period of the eighteenth and nineteenth centuries, when the use of generalized political humor was found most broadly among the more educated classes. In the twentieth century, and so far in the current century, there has been a massive widespread emergence of political humor enjoyed by different classes and social groups. This widening democratization and enjoyment of political humor corresponds to the growing importance of the so-called middle classes. A numerical majority and homogeneous in social and cultural terms, they share a similar disposition toward humor (Kuipers 2001). Furthermore, the consensus among focus group respondents concerning the use of political humor in the media (including programs that deal with violent issues) is positive. This is because such shows target allegedly controversial content and simply make it funny. Thus, our society creates a distance between real problems and media discussion. Humor is a basic resource whose function is, to paraphrase Walter Benjamin, a certain "aestheticization" of politics (1968). When people think of political humor, even those instances addressing issues of violence, they supposedly believe that humor is healthy, therapeutic, and part of a positive energy that connects with the playful nature of human beings and the freedom of opinion manifest in calm, tolerant, and modern societies.[2] Humor is something that tends to create a pleasurable and unrestrained social ambiance. Serving mainly to entertain, humor is free from any political purpose, so that any topic is susceptible to humorous expression (Davies 1990; Palmer 1994; Rappoport 2005). Its definitive success is ultimately linked not so much to control and censorship of political power but rather its ability to connect with the free market of appreciative applause.

In the analysis of humor, there is a second theoretical perspective that contradicts the alleged benefits of its therapeutic virtues. This perspective insists on analyzing how political humor circulating in our society is primarily a political tool, a construction elaborated in social settings and utilized to mock and ridicule an intended object[3] Jean Paul Sartre's assertion in his famous essay *Portrait of the Antisemite* argues against the conventional image of anti-Semites as being rigid and humorless. Instead, he paints them as people who are able to connect in a socially acceptable communal ethnic, national, and religious hatred—united with a sense of humor (1946). This reveals a side to the phenomenon of political humor that is dissimilar from before, less affable and more disturbing (España 2000; Husband 1988). Political humor appears rather as a violent mecha-

---

2. The list of authors who have studied humor from a positive perspective in the various academic disciplines, especially the social sciences, psychology, and cognitive linguistics, is enormous. Among many others, the following should be noted: Attardo (1994); Berger (1997); Davies (1990, 2002); Fry (1963, 2002); Haig (1988); Idígoras (2002); Oring (2003); Raskin (1985, 1998); Sloane (2001); Stallybrass and White (1997).

3. The list of authors who pose a more critical view of humor is equally wide. Among many others, the following should be noted: Billig (2001a, 2001b, 2005); Dundes (1987); Dundes and Hauschild (1988); Ford (2000); Holmes (2000); Lewis (1997, 2006); Lockyer and Pickering (2001, 2005); Mulkay (1988); Paton and Powell (1988); Paton, Powell, and Wagg (1996); Willis (2003).

nism capable of creating sociopolitical divisions and hierarchies. In this
way, it reflects the political order of society, and the fine line between what
is laughable and what is taboo among those who laugh and those who suffer (Boskin 1990).

The hypothesis explored in this chapter is that the Basque television
program *Vaya Semanita*, especially during its first two seasons (2003–
2005), was perceived more in line with the first theoretical perspective,
although both theoretical angles are plausible and frame an interesting
debate. Presumably, the impact of this television program in those years,
according to the answers of the participants in my fieldwork, could be
understood not only as a success of humor when talking about Basque
politics in general, and terrorism in particular, but also as the victory of
a particular political discourse—one that was more relaxed, less tense,
and served to reinforce a particular image of Basque politics and terrorist
violence and at a very specific political moment. From a formal standpoint, the program uses a modern audiovisual format that is energetic,
lighthearted, linguistically informal, and sufficiently apolitical to suit the
tastes of any social group or ideology. However, substantively, the program was perceived in a less neutral light than might have been revealed
at first glance. In fact, arguably, it is no coincidence that *Vaya Semanita*
made a significant change at the end of its second season, which coincided
not only with the resignation of the initial program team, led by comedian
Oscar Terol (2005–2006), but also with the holding of Basque regional
elections in May 2005. These elections in themselves were, together with
the Spanish general elections of March 2004, the beginnings of a series
of changes to Basque political life (Llera 2005). Here, I argue that both
the ludic and political theoretical perspectives used to analyze this type
of comedy show are complementary, but not necessarily symmetrical in
importance.

To test this hypothesis, our methodology involved conducting five
focus groups with students from different social and political profiles in
order to analyze social discourse concerning the image and content of
Vaya Semanita in its first two seasons.[4] The following information will be

---

4. The fieldwork for this research was conducted from 2005 to 2007. Four variables were
considered important for the selection of focus group participants: (1) the degree of knowledge
of the program *Vaya Semanita*, (2) the degree of appreciation of this type of comedy program,
(3) the degree of closeness to the Basque Country, and (4) the ideological orientation. Of the
five focus groups conducted, four were on the campus of the University of the Basque Country
with students from the Faculty of Social Sciences and Communication. The other groups were

analyzed in four sections: (1) the first discusses the overall assessment of the program and its alleged ideological character; (2) the second examines the relationship between the target audience and the program's objective and creators/subjects; (3) the third examines the program's contents; and finally, (4) the fourth section discusses the role of such a program as a means to understanding politics in a modern society such as the Basque Country.

Vaya Semanita: Revolutionary, Conservative, or Nationalist?

The emergence of *Vaya Semanita* on Basque public television was considered a revolutionary act even though the ruling political party in the Basque Country at that time (and for previous decades), the Basque Nationalist Party (EAJ-PNV by its Basque and Spanish acronyms), was located in the conservative ideological, nationalist, and center-right political spectrum. This apparent paradox is important when assessing the arguments made by participants in focus groups regarding the alleged ideological focus of the program (Wilson 1990). Historically, political humor has been associated with left-wing liberal groups, with the assumption that they are more likely to press and encourage the use of corrosive, subversive, or uninhibited humor, as compared to traditional norms (Kercher 2006). By contrast, people located within the conservative ideological spectrum are supposedly more reactionary toward political humor because it assumes a dangerous contradiction with the maintenance of order and set values (Saroglou 2002). This romantic conceit is inherited from times when humor was associated with some heroism in the struggle for freedom and democracy. Today, this is a myth that hardly holds empirically (Asa Berger 1996, 27). As many authors have suggested, we should analyze to what extent the opposite view is actually more accurate. In other words, the "humoristic method" of communication is, in itself, a practice that seeks to accommodate a conservative vision within the sociopolitical status quo (Mulkay 1988).

As focus group participants pointed out, one of the "revolutionary" attributes of *Vaya Semanita* was its breaking of a taboo that had been present, which was more or less implicit, in the audiovisual media of the

---

conducted at the Center for Basque Studies at the University of Nevada, Reno, United States, with students who were minimally knowledgeable of Basque culture. In the text, the discussion groups are cited indicating, first, the group number and, second, the number of the participant. Thus, GD3/gd1 is the person assigned the number 1 in focus group number 3.

Basque Country—the comic taboo pertaining to political issues, and especially terrorism:

> (1) "People accepted and liked *Vaya Semanita* a lot, especially in the first
> few seasons. This is because for the first time a television program por-
> trayed Basque people in a humorous light, how they actually live with
> their problems. This dose of humor softens the problems which for many
> years have plagued the Basque Country" (GT3/gt6).
>
> (2) "In *Vaya Semanita*, comedians portray taboo topics, but with a hint
> of satire and humor. This fine touch of humor deftly treats what could
> otherwise be a trauma" (GT3/gt2).
>
> (3) "Programs like *Vaya Semanita* do not depoliticize the population, but
> rather the opposite. . . . One could have less serious programs that are
> more entertaining and enjoyable. Usually, politicians are out of reach of
> the population, and it is through these programs that the populace gets to
> participate and gets involved in politics at a time that when disaffection is
> a virus in democracy" (GT1/gt5).
>
> (4) "To say that political humor is frivolous politics seems mistaken. The
> fact that something will help to cool or to slacken the political preferences
> of citizens through smiles or laughter is something to be welcomed. In
> fact, laughter is a good approach toward politics, since it seeks to turn
> concepts on their heads" (GT5/gt3).

In these excerpts, it is evident that one of the innovative objectives of the
program was precisely trying to *depoliticize* political issues—especially
thorny ones such as violence—by removing any language that might generate a dehumanization of any group or political situation, so that later a key
repoliticization occurred through humor (see quotations 3 and 4). Interestingly, comments that emphasized the idea that the humorous treatment
of political violence in programs like this make sense to the extent that the
political context was "more relaxed," given the fall of ETA terrorist activity
in recent years (see quotation 1). If the political tension prompted by the
terrorist attacks had decreased, participants said, one might then ask, what
could be the cause of opposition to this new, lighthearted, humorous, and
relaxed vision of Basque politics? The arguments of some people object-
ing to *Vaya Semanita*'s humor relating to political violence issues were in
the minority. These comments were viewed with suspicion by the rest of
the study's participants who questioned if such opinions were enacted to
decisively politicize the program's vision. In fact, as shown in the following
quote, the more or less critical voices resorted to proleptic arguments or
ideas based on long anticipatory explanations in order to justify a posi-

tion, knowing that this position was identified with a social minority. In view of quotation 5 below, we could say that one result of the program was to thwart any "revolutionary" attempt to seriously politicize Basque political opinion:

> (5) "I think in a situation as serious as we are experiencing one cannot make wisecracks or jokes, because all you are doing is hiding behind a screen that covers up real life situations in which people have lived, and which no one could say was good. Very often, you forget the bad times and laugh at them; I usually find myself doing it. However, seeing it on television, conveyed with irony, makes you think the only way to address this issue is through these means. I don't know . . . but hey, this is just my personal opinion. Although I do know that ultimately this type of program, I suppose, is downplaying the times we live in" (GT4/gt2).

Vaya Semanita and Its Viewers

The viewers of *Vaya Semanita* are a further key to understanding the success of the program. It is widely accepted that every joke usually has two kinds of recipients: those who are invited to laugh and those who are the target of the humor. The former belong to the social group that uses these practices to reaffirm its majority position. The latter, by contrast, are those who "suffer" to some extent the consequences of said humor, thereby reflecting their peripheral status.[5] Following the classification proposed by Christie Davies, one of the world's leading scholars on humor, dominant humor in all societies emerges for two reasons: due to "ridiculously dim-witted" behavior or "suspiciously canny" behavior (1990, 2002). The question, therefore, is to see how different actors position themselves according to their place in Basque society. In view of the opinions of the individuals who participated in the focus groups, the students more sympathetic to the ruling party's (the EAJ-PNV) ideological sensibility were the people most talked about in all group discussion. Additionally, they gave a positive opinion on the "therapeutic" benefits of the program. Moreover, individuals who had no particular ideological identification—those for whom the program was "just entertainment"—were of a similar

---

5. The term "suffering" as related to the topic of humor must be clearly differentiated from other social practices and policies that actually produce physical and material pain. As Christie Davies (1990, 8) notes, one must not confuse jokes and genuine aggression, given that it is difficult to ascertain how humor devalues and trivializes the importance of causes that really do generate social pain.

opinion. In general, when asked who the potential target users were, most viewers shared the widespread impression that the program was intended for everyone.[6] As shown in the following views, however, the groups also provided some significant nuances:

(9) "*Vaya Semanita* has become a benchmark that has managed to place politics in the service of laughter without any subterfuge. The political left, right, nationalists, and even terrorists or the police may be the targets of these comedians. In the vast majority of cases, they have managed to make people smile without ruffling too many feathers . . . and if they do this to the most radical on either side, then maybe the humor is even more successful. . . . After all, humor, in the end, can not only serve to broaden or solidify information, but also to connect the population via a cohesive kind of humor" (GT1/gt5).

(10) "Much of the program's success lies not in mockery of the Basque County, but in identification with it. I mean that the vast majority of viewers identify with the situations and characteristics of the particular social groups that are presented. Either way, we identify with the situations reflected in the characters and their personal traits, and although we do not see ourselves identified, we do see a friend or family member embodied in them" (GT2/gt1).

(11) "The program *Vaya Semanita* has changed its brand of comedy following the change of government in Madrid. The first seasons were funnier. So, we might ask why? In my opinion, the entity being ridiculed before [referring to the PP, Partido Popular/People's Party] was when discourse in society was more serious, more radical. So when this situation was ridiculed, everyone thought it was funnier" (GT2/gt2).

(12) "The debate is not whether the humor was appropriate. The point is that in a liberal society, if you don't love it, you don't buy it. It's another thing entirely when humor creates certain xenophobic attitudes. One might say that both forms of humor work in the same way, often inseparably. In the case of *Vaya Semanita*, the aim of the humor was rather to ridicule the [conservative] group that was in power, the very same group who had laughed in different ways at radical Basque nationalists, socialists, and the masses" (GT2/gt3).

---

6. At this juncture, it is interesting to note that ETB was the most important media and information source in virtually every social group, according to survey data from Euskobarometro concerning the years 2003 to 2005, as ascertained via discussion groups in 2005 to 2007. The only exceptions in this case were the supporters of the PP (Partido Popular, People's Party) in the Basque Country, only a minority of whom recognized Basque public television as their medium of reference.

(13) "While it is true that *Vaya Semanita* is a program that is broadcast on ETB, I do not think its goal is to benefit the EAJ-PNV but rather it seeks to ease the tensions of the social climate in the Basque Country, toying with the perennial conflict through satirical and sarcastic humor that pokes fun at all the poles that exist in society, from Basque nationalists to Spanish nationalists. The truth is that making fun of it all tends to parody both extremes, giving very little latitude with regard to either the EAJ-PNV or PSE [Partido Socialista de Euskadi, Socialist Party of the Basque Country]" (GT3/gt2).

Following Davies's thesis, in focus groups, students sympathetic to the moderate nationalist parties in power and those more apolitical or moderate are the social groups that could be considered the normal majority to which the humor of the program targets. They are considered the groups who primarily generate consensus on what is laughable in the community. They are the people who "are not at extremes," and who do not consider themselves "dim-witted" or "canny," but simply enjoy the humor in a neutral manner, without being "radicalized" by it. They are the kind of people who do not make jokes because they identify with humorous parody, "even though we ourselves are not ourselves reflected in what we see." This is the population for which the program and its brand of parody is primarily, though not exclusively, intended.

The arguments emerging from focus groups that identified more with the PP, radical Basque nationalism, and the PSE were somewhat different from sentiments previously declared. This begs the question: to what extent do their statements correspond to a different target profile entirely? In these cases, their basic approach was to say that the program's political humor was "basically entertaining" (as stated more frequently by the supporters of radical Basque nationalism and the PSE, and much less so in the case of PP supporters, who considered it "basically boring"). However, they also stated that some of the program's sentiments tended to have some political overtones, especially in terms of terrorism, which they did not like very much. In the case of students close to the PP, all indicated that the PP was one of the main targets of political ridicule in the program. As will be seen in more detail, the PP somehow represented the "canny group" par excellence. In other words, the PP is the allegedly astute social group that the playful storyline of the program suspiciously casts as wanting to change, from its position of power, the collective imagination of the Basque community. In the case of radical Basque nationalist supporters, they pointed out that the parodies concerning their social group referred to their "extreme" social position even though the mockery alleged the "dim-wittedness" of their violent actions. Some acknowledged that they even considered it funny. Finally, in the case of students sympathizing with the PSE, their position was more ambivalent, given that some of their critiques corresponded with radical Basque nationalism and the PP. In general, however, they were more in tune with the moderate position that strayed away from the extremes of "Basque independence and Spanish nationalism." In a way, as I will show, the PSE was in a way ridiculed by its absence, because the program did not link it to "dim-wittedness" or "cunning," something that a few socialist sympathizers found humorous because they identified this with their own political experience.

One of the issues discussed by participants was the statement indicating that the program had been successful because it "ridicules all political parties equally." Despite the generality of this statement, some participants, especially the supporters of radical Basque nationalism and the PP, were unwilling to accept it at face value. For them, the assumption that the humor of the program established a certain symmetry between all social groups and all subjects was a somewhat misleading argument. In the following quotations, two people with opposing ideological profiles, manifest their opinions:

(14) "In the first two seasons the program sought to ridicule the PP and HB [Herri Batasuna, the radical Basque nationalist party]. Ridiculing the PP did not pose a danger, because at that time it was in power in Madrid. After, the state elections of 2004, however, things changed when the PSOE [Spanish Socialist Party] won in Madrid. When this occurred, there was no point ridiculing the PP, as it was no longer the governing party. So, they were forced to change the line of the program, increasingly ridiculing themselves, that is, the EAJ-PNV. In my opinion, this is a way of bringing politics into society, but always from the perspective of who controls it, that is, the EAJ-PNV. . . . Apart from this, another objective of the program was to introduce a particular way of narrating events through humor. This can be seen, for example, in the constant distinction between the Basque Country and Spain, which shows the strong nationalist presence in the program. It was an attempt to normalize a discourse that in reality brought out a lot of controversy" (GT3/gt3).

(15) "From the beginning, the program *Vaya Semanita* intended to strengthen the position of the Basque government. Why else would they allow such a program on a network that basically they manage?" (GT4/gt5).

The key to these arguments lies in an appeal to the process of creating *Vaya Semanita*. This is not so much a debate about viewers, but about the individuals who are actually producing the program. It is no coincidence that those who most identified with radical Basque nationalism and the PP made specific mention in their statements as to the source of this program and the governing party, the EAJ-PNV, as a key discursive position to justify their criticism of this kind of humor. It is clear that this way of politicizing the program revealed an attempt to discredit the alleged creator of the humor, the EAJ-PNV. In the opinion of the individual cited above, *Vaya Semanita* was not so much Basque humor made for the Basque people, but rather humor about a particular group of Basques—a humor that ridiculed all social groups, yet not all equally. Thus, it revealed a hierarchical position of each group, depending on the perspective of who created the subject of humor.

The Content of *Vaya Semanita*

The structure and program content of *Vaya Semanita* faithfully represents a dominant type of humor in modern societies. In other words, it presents a type of humor that traverses institutionalized spaces, mainly in the media, and is equipped with a typical framework in which humorous practices are organized serially, minimizing the originality of the contents, which are often subject to formal and repetitive structures (Taylor 1988; Pye 2006; Wagg 1996). The political humor in *Vaya Semanita* is basically a highly institutionalized humor; it is unidirectional, hierarchical, and formal according to the classification of the different spaces of humor outlined by Michael J. Mulkay (1988, 152–78), who situates humor in relation to how far it is institutionalized. This means that the humor is based on socially recognizable topics, amplified by weekly repeated gags and scripts without spectator participation. Obviously, this format facilitates control of the humorous content and permits scripts to follow predictable patterns.

According to the responses in virtually all the discussion groups in which participants were aware of the program, one of *Vaya Semanita*'s greatest moments was a series of sketches involving Los Santxez (the Sanchez family). These were based on a Spanish immigrant family from Salamanca who had come to live in the Basque Country.[7] The sketches tell

---

7. In fact, one of the "comic objectives" in this sketch was how the Spanish family, originally known as The Sanchezes (in Spanish spelling), could become a Basque family by changing the spelling of their name to The Santxezes, reflecting the Basque-language spelling and pronunciation.

their story with humorous tag lines and a repetitive structure that is easy for the public to grasp. These antics were repeated monotonously in each show ad nauseam. It is important to note that this series, displaying one of the largest political contents of the program, disappeared at the end of the second season in 2005, despite being one of the most successful and best remembered by the audience:

> (16) "It is difficult to get the big picture of the Basque Country when you live here, and *Vaya Semanita* has enabled many to have a vision of Basque society more in tune with reality, such as the Sanchez family from Salamanca with one son in the Ertzaintza [Basque police force] and another who is a radical nationalist. In other words, these are faithful recreations of Basque society" (GT4/gt4).
>
> (17) "*Vaya Semanita* targets a diverse social spectrum; it seeks to reach the different political sectors. It transmits an image that I think is normal, or normal in the sense that nationalism is present in institutions, as two sides of the same coin, as is inherent to the nature of Basque self-governance. Its main function is to exaggerate real life, and that viewed from the perspective of politics, which leads to a dumbing down of political debates. Just like the response given by the mother from the Sanchez family when she was asked for whom they voted: 'the same ones, that's all'" (GT3/gt1).
>
> (18) "One of the moments I most used to look forward to came in a sketch of the the Sanchez family. The heart of it was how they made fun of the PP father" (GT2/gt3).

The sketch series "Los Santxez" was, in all likelihood, the single most successful of the program. The family consisted of four members: the father (Pepe), the mother (Mari), and two sons (the eldest, Patxi, and the youngest, Antxon). The structure of the sketches was fashioned around four characters allegedly representing the four organizations that span the Basque Country's political spectrum, the EAJ-PNV, PSE, PP, and radical Basque nationalists. In the sketches each week, they interacted comically in reflecting current political news. In focus groups, one of the issues noted by the participants was their identification with the imparted political sensitivities of each of the members of the family, taking into consideration of course—as participants more or less agreed—that the sketches contained a sort of "political evaluation." The issue of political violence and terrorism was, in fact, one of the central elements of familial tension.

It is significant then that the vast majority of participants in focus groups claimed that the most ridiculous character in the family (and the one who aroused more laughter from viewers, as much for his politics as for his hysterical attitude toward Basque terrorist violence) was the father, who is clearly identified as a PP voter. The next character whose ideology was equally evident and laughable was the youngest son, Antxon. He is unmistakably identified with radical Basque nationalism and ridiculed for his rather naive and impish defense of the use of violence for political ends. The eldest is a police officer for the Basque police force and reads the newspaper *Deia* (a newspaper empathetic to the EAJ-PNV). Participants in focus groups stated that what made this character humorous was the way he represented "political order"—in other words, he took pleasure in exercising legitimate violence by political power. The final character, the mother (the only woman in the family), was in a more unique position, if possible. Although supposedly close to the PSE, she was ideologically indeterminate. The mother emerged in the discussion groups as the character who most clearly opposed any justification of violence. Interestingly, this sort of common sense provoked less laughter among the participants. One could argue that the success of the "Los Santxez" format (as noted in quotation 16) was based on its ability to reproduce what was then considered as a credible family prototype. Though exaggerated, it diversely parodied the Basque political spectrum: a family of Spanish nationalist parents who migrate to the Basque Country and have Basque nationalist children, one of them linked to ETA violence and the other fighting against it as a police officer. The fact is, however, that the disappearance of the PP after March 2004, with the loss of the general elections in Spain, made a narrative that parodied and exaggerated nationalism to the point of ridicule harder in the new Basque imaginary. And this paralleled a new strategy of peaceful opposition proposed by new Spanish PSOE prime minister José Luis Rodríguez Zapatero that concerned various initiatives in Basque politics, such as the Plan Ibarretxe and the fight against terrorism.[8] As stated by several students in the groups, "Los Santxez" disappeared from the show in 2005 because "something was missing." That "something" was surely the lack of real conflict between the stereotypes of the PP and Basque nationalism in Basque political life. Given this absence, the humor had lost much of its appeal.

---

8. One of the most important debates in the Basque Country and Spain during these years was the reform of the Law of Autonomy in the Basque Country, popularly known as Plan Ibarretxe, in reference to the Basque *lehendakari* (president) Juan Jose Ibarretxe (EAJ-PNV), the driving force of the reform.

The Role of *Vaya Semanita* in Basque Politics

The fourth and final deliberation among the focus groups was to assess the role that this type of comedy show had in democratic societies such as the Basque Country. The problem of censorship is especially problematic when it pertains to political violence and the representation of victims of terrorism, which was one of the recurrent themes among the groups. Likewise, this topic is addressed in much of the humor studies literature (Davies 1996). As quotation 19 reflects, and as found in most of the groups, there is a notion that political humor maintains a profoundly constructive relationship that is connected to freedom of expression and the design of democracy. Thus, any call for potential censorship should, in principle, be criticized:

(19) "The kind of political humor and satire allowed is indicative of the level of democracy and freedom of expression of a country. A country that does not accept humorous criticism on certain topics means that its level of freedom is reduced. There are artists who endeavor, in different ways, to introduce political humor in society, but soon fall under the power of censorship. Either way, the natural environment for humor is democracy" (GT5/gt1).

(20) "*Vaya Semanita* illustrates everyday situations in a humorous and exaggerated way, but it also sets limits. There is no humor concerning the victims of ETA, not because they do not exist, but because there are misgivings about the effect this would have on viewers and at a political level. The same applies to the role that is given to the *batasunis* [a parody of Sesame Street puppets, portrayed here as radical nationalists] or that of *kale* [*borroka*, low-level politicized violence and vandalism]. There is no room for humor in relation to arrests, torture, and imprisonment. . . . These limits go beyond simply maintaining an audience. What if the above issues were to become the subject of humor? *Vaya Semanita* cannot escape the control and censorship of its financiers. This phenomenon occurs today in all media, without exception" (GT4/gt2).

(21) "There is an issue that still haunts our society, that is the victims of terrorism—and to cast it humorously is complicated, if not even more violent. As a follower of the program, I do not remember any engagement with this topic. Maybe it's a subject that is very difficult to speak about, but having breached the topics of ETA and gays in the Civil Guard, one shouldn't be so squeamish. Surely, soon enough, this topic will arise in serious, and not so serious, programs" (GT3/gt6).

The problem of censorship in comedy shows is related to debates about the limits of these types of practices. As quotation 20 reflects, respondents raised concerns about the need for some level of censorship or self-censorship in this type of program—pertaining not only to *Vaya Semanita* but also to a general level when addressing certain issues, especially those related to terrorism. It is interesting to note, however, that the majority opinion in the groups, as indicated in quotation 21, recognized that political humor is, by definition, expansive in content and format, so any attempt to impose censorship on humorous practices is difficult to justify. Likewise, as noted in a recent study on the use of humor in the Netherlands, the degree of inhibition along with the existence of a more aggressive ruthlessness in dealing with issues prone to humorous depiction (such as happens with terrorism) is correlated with the degree of tolerance, individualization, and secularization of society. Arguably, this allows for greater acceptance of this type of humor (Kuipers 2001, 145). In the Basque case, the narratives of the participants in focus groups ranged from a theoretical recognition of the existence of some kind of censorship to a specific recognition of a trend in our societies toward a *hyper-humorization* of any subject, which in theory should not be negative.

Moreover, one last perception that ran through the focus groups was the notion of the risks that such programs have when it came to projecting a certain depoliticization of public debate. As stated in quotation 22, although these programs are positive because freedom of expression is a fundamental value in illuminating and analyzing problems, they may also contribute to a trivialization of critical public attitudes in society. In other words, the excessive ridicule inherent in the program could be seen as equally detrimental as the excessive seriousness of those respondents who argued that within the show's subject matter truly important things were at stake:

> (22) "Political humor works to show problems, but that is it. If society resorts only to mockery and derision of the problem, it never faces it. It's good that we laugh at the problems of housing, the economy, and terrorism . . . but this is nothing more than venting. Keep in mind that problems are not fixed by themselves, save for a need to change. If we expect the final push to come from politicians because they are pressured by humor, then we're in real trouble" (GT3/gt6).

The paradox of allegedly frivolous infotainment programs like *Vaya Semanita* is that, in reality, they have helped to show a democratic maturity in Basque society concerning sensitive issues such as political violence and terrorism. They have also served to reinforce the idea that in a truly liberal and democratic society the comic treatment of any subject can expand in proportion to a diminishing fear of free expression. Although there is a risk that humor could replace crucial conversations pertaining to issues in the media (such the issue of victims of terrorism), the truth is that the use of humor may help to better contextualize genuine understanding within society.

Conclusions

An analysis of the information obtained from focus groups suggests that *Vaya Semanita* possesses similar features to programs viewed elsewhere, but it also renders specific features particular to the dynamics of the Basque Country. My first observation noted that the novelty of this program in 2003, along with the state of Basque society at a time when it was democratically more mature (with respectively low levels of terrorist violence), were the main reasons that contributed to a public medium like Basque public television's ability to "report" on sensitive issues. Utilizing a comic approach, it generated high ratings and became a genuine social phenomenon.

The second observation dealt with the structure, content, and viewership of the program. As Davies argues, in all societies in which ethnic, cultural, religious, or partisan differences exist, humor is built on stereotypes that reflect and reinforce certain asymmetric and dominant ideas that such humor exploits. The program *Vaya Semanita*, in this sense, is not an exception. It does not create new stereotypes or provoke social or political change. Rather, its success lies in its ability to take advantage of the existence of a particular Basque political imaginary. Through this specific view of Basque political reality, legitimized by majority opinion, it somehow reinforces these stereotypes and turns them into comedy. Any comedy show with political connotations works successfully by means of caricatures and stereotypes that are recognizable to the public and seen as fair targets by most people. These are manifest in two forms: the stereotype of the "dim-witted" and the "canny" individual. In this case, as recognized by the focus group participants, the humor of the program between 2003 and 2005 worked to the extent that its viewers detected these stereotypes. For example, there was the case of ridiculing the "canny," which was directed at the PP (seen as a threat to the identity of the Basque community). In addition, to a lesser extent, there were instances of ridiculing the "dim-witted," directed at Basque nationalists (who were seen as a threat to the good image of the Basque community). The most prevalent parallel in most of the focus group participants' narratives was to defend the program as playful and harmless. This was accomplished by reaffirming the mocking and the stereotypes, both political and nonpolitical, that were offered in search of a comic evaluation of reality. In turn, the reactions of participants who said they were upset with some of the comic elements, especially on issues related to violence and terrorism, came in two forms. On the one hand, there were those trying to laugh at themselves, so as not to increase the level of ridicule directed toward them . On the other hand, there were those trying to seriously criticize the show's creators and warn of the dangers of trivializing political issues. This second opinion only demonstrated a certain vulnerability when it came to understanding the use of a humorous stereotype in which there is no means to control it.

In sum, as noted in the initial hypothesis of this research, the program *Vaya Semanita* was perceived by most people in our discussion groups as a comedy show and not as a political program. This did not preclude some political interpretations of the show, especially by those persons more sensitive and closer to certain issues, such as terrorist violence. This made their evaluation and interpretation of the program much more complex. In fact, in these cases, a liking for the humor mixed with a disaffection for the same humor that, in some ways, was perceived to have been made by others.

References

Asa Berger, Arthur. 1996. "The Politics of Laughter." In *The Social Faces of Humour: Practices and Issues*, edited by George Paton, Chris Powell, and Stephen Wagg. Aldershot, UK: Ashgate Publishing.

Attardo, Salvatore. 1994. *Linguistic Theories of Humor*. Berlin: Mouton de Gruyter.

Baum, Matthew A. 2003: "Soft News and Political Knowledge: Evidence of Absence or Absence of Evidence?" *Political Communication* 20, no. 2: 173–90.

Benjamin, Walter. 1968. "The Work of Art in the Age of Mechanical Reproduction." In *Illuminations: Essays and Reflections*, edited and with an introduction by Hannah Arendt. Translated by Harry Zohn. New York: Schocken Books.

Berger, Peter L. 1997. *Redeeming Laughter: The Comic Dimension of Human Experience.* Berlin: Walter de Gruyter.

Billig, Michael. 2001a. "Humour and Embarrassment: Limits of 'Nice-Guy' Theories of Social Life." *Theory, Culture and Society* 18, no. 5: 23–43.

———. 2001b. "Humour and Hatred: The Racist Jokes of the Ku Klux Klan." *Discourse and Society* 12, no. 3: 267–89.

———. 2005. *Laughter and Ridicule: Towards a Social Critique of Humour.* London: Sage.

Boskin, Joseph. 1990. "American Political Humor: Touchables and Taboos." *International Political Science Review* 11, no. 4: 473–82.

Davies, Christie. 1990. *Ethnic Humor around the World: A Comparative Analysis.* Bloomington: Indiana University Press.

———. 1996. "Puritanical and Politically Correct? A Critical Historical Account of Changes in the Censorship of Comedy by the BBC." In *The Social Faces of Humour: Practices and Issues*, edited by George Paton, Chris Powell, and Stephen Wagg. Aldershot, UK: Ashgate Publishing.

———. 2002. *The Mirth of Nations.* New Brunswick, NJ: Transaction Publishers.

Dundes, Alan. 1987. *Cracking Jokes: Studies of Sick Humor Cycles and Stereotypes.* Berkeley, CA: Ten Speed Press.

Dundes, Alan, and Thomas Hauschild. 1988. "Auschwitz Jokes." In *Humour in Society: Resistance and Control*, edited by George Paton and Chris Powell. London: Macmillan.

España, Ramón de. 2000. *El odio: Fuente de vida y motor del mundo.* Barcelona: Ediciones Martínez Roca.

Ford, Thomas. 2000. "Effects of Sexist Humor on Tolerance of Sexist Events." *Personality and Social Psychology Bulletin* 26, no. 9: 1094–1107.

Fry, William. 1963. *Sweet Madness: A Study of Humor.* Palo Alto, CA: Pacific Books.

———. 2002. "Humor and the Brain: A Selective Review." *Humor* 15, no. 3: 305–33.

Haig, Robin Andrew. 1988. *The Anatomy of Humor: Biopsychosocial and Therapeutic Perspectives.* Springfield, IL: Thomas.

Holmes, Janet. 2000. "Politeness, Power and Provocation: How Humour Functions in the Workplace." *Discourse Studies* 2, no. 2: 159–85.

Husband, Charles. 1988. "Racist Humour and Racist Ideology in British Television, or I Laughed Till You Cried." In *Humour in Society: Resistance and Control*, edited by George Paton and Chris Powell. London: Macmillan.

Idígoras, Angel Rodríguez. 2002. *El valor terapéutico del humor*. Bilbao: Desclee de Brouwer.

Kercher, Stephen E. 2006. *Revel with a Cause: Liberal Satire in Postwar America*. Chicago: University of Chicago Press.

Kuipers, Giselinde. 2001. *Good Humor, Bad Taste: A Sociology of the Joke*. Berlin: Mouton de Gruyter.

Lewis, Paul. 1997. "The Killing Jokes of the American Eighties." *Humor* 10, no. 3: 251–83.

———. 2006. *Cracking Up: American Humor in a Time of Conflict*. Chicago: University of Chicago Press.

Llera, Francisco José. 2005. "Pluralismo y moderación: Las elecciones vascas de 2005." *Cuadernos de Alzate* 32: 181–202.

Lockyer, Sharon, and Michael J. Pickering. 2001. "Dear Shit-Shovellers: Humour, Censure and the Discourse of Complaint." *Discourse and Society* 12, no. 5: 633–51.

———, eds. 2005. *Beyond a Joke: The Limits of Humour*. London: Palgrave Macmillan.

Mulkay, Michael J. 1988. *On Humour: Its Nature and Its Place in Modern Society*. Cambridge, UK: Polity Press.

Oring, Elliot. 2003. *Engaging Humor*. Urbana: University of Illinois Press.

Palmer, Jerry. 1994. *Taking Humour Seriously*. London: Routledge.

Paton, George, and Chris Powell, eds. 1988. *Humour in Society: Resistance and Control*. London: Macmillan.

Paton, George, Chris Powell, and Stephen Wagg, eds. 1996. *The Social Faces of Humour: Practices and Issues*. Aldershot, UK: Ashgate Publishing.

Pye, Gillian. 2006. "Comedy Theory and the Postmodern." *Humor* 19, no. 1: 53–70.

Rappoport, Leon. 2005. *Punchlines: The Case for Racial, Ethnic, and Gender Humor*. Westport, CT: Praeger Publishers.

Raskin, Viktor. 1985. *Semantic Mechanisms of Humor*. Hingham, MA: Reidel Publishing Company.

———. 1998. "The Sense of Humor and Truth." In *The Sense of Humor: Explorations of a Personality Characteristic*, edited by Willibald Ruch. Berlin: Mouton de Gruyter.

Saroglou, Vassilis. 2002. "Religion and Sense of Humor: An A Priori Incompatibility? Theoretical Considerations from a Psychological Perspective." *Humor* 15, no. 2: 191–214.

Sartre, Jean Paul. 1946. *Portrait of the Antisemite*. New York: Partisan Review.

Sloane, Arthur A. 2001. *Humor in the White House: The Wit of Five American Presidents*. Jefferson, NC: McFarland Press.

Sloterdijk, Peter. 2000. *Normas para el parque humano: Una respuesta a la Carta sobre el Humanismo de Heidegger*. Translated by Teresa Rocha Barco. Madrid: Siruela. German version: *Reglen für den Menschenpark: Ein Antwortschreiben zum Brief über den Humanismos*. Frankfurt: Suhrkamp, 1999.

Stallybrass, Peter, and Allon White. 1997. *From Carnival to Transgression: The Subcultures Reader*. London: Routledge.

Taylor, Paul. 1988. "Scriptwriters and Producers: A Dimension of Control in Television Situation Comedies." In *Humour in Society: Resistance and Control*, edited by George Paton and Chris Powell. London: Macmillan.

Terol, Oscar. 2005. *Todos nacemos vascos*. Madrid: Aguilar.

———. 2006. *Ponga un vasco en su vida*. Madrid: Aguilar.

Wagg, Stephen. 1996. "Everything Else Is Propaganda: The Politics of Alternative Comedy." In *The Social Faces of Humour: Practices and Issues*, edited by George Paton, Chris Powell, and Stephen Wagg. Aldershot, UK: Ashgate Publishing.

Willis, Clint, ed. 2003. *The I Hate Republicans Reader: Why the GOP Is Totally Wrong about Everything*. New York: Thunder's Month Press.

Wilson, Glenn. 1990. "Ideology and Humor Preferences." *International Political Science Review* 11, no. 4: 461–72.

Index

14–17; victims of, 105–27; as whitewasher, 36–39; against women, 8. *see also* conflict; ETA attacks

violent conflict. *see* conflict; violence

violent events, 20n

violent incidents, 20n

visualization, 18

vocabulary: of extermination, 43–44; propagandistic terms, 152

W

Wachowski brothers, 30

Wacquant, Loïc, 45–46

war: motivations that can lead to, 75; risk factors, 75

war movies, 31n

Weerasethakul, Apichatpong, 61

Welles, Orson, 30

white hands (symbol), 143

Why We Fight, 21n

Wolf, Naomi, 58–59

women: in conflict situations, 89; definition of, 67; images of, 68; invisibility of, 51–69; as material without sufficient form, 55; as sexual beings, 59; violence against, 8

Women's Institute (Image Observatory of Spain), 65, 66

workshops on war-related issues, 88–89

World Bank, 74, 82

World Trade Center, 18

World War II, 21n, 35, 39, 40

Wuxia genre, 30

Wyrzykowski family, 36

X

Xbox, 29n

Y

Ybarra, Javier de, 137

Yemen, 83–84

Yimou, Zhang, 30, 30n

Yo soy Betty, la fea, 56

YouTube, 20

Z

Zapatero, José Luis Rodríguez, 183

Zapruder, Abraham, 20

Zapruder film, 20, 21, 29n

Zaragoza, Spain, 140

Zaratamo (Bizkaia), 139

Zelig, 24–25

ZEN Plan, 150n

zero image, 19

List of Contributors

For full biographical information about the contributors, links to their projects, and more, visit www.basque.unr.edu/currentresearch/contributors.

José Ignacio Armentia
Carmen Arocena
José María Caminos
Miguel Ángel Casado
Juan de Dios Uriarte
Alfonso Dubois
Ramón Esparza
Carmelo Garitaonandia
Maialen Garmendia
Gemma Martínez
Jose Antonio Mingolarra
Carmelo Moreno
Nekane Parejo
Imanol Zubero
Nekane E. Zubiaur
Imanol Zumalde